RUMI

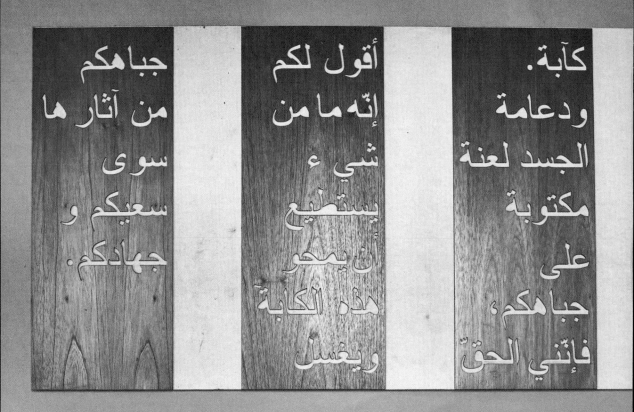

This book is a gift to the generation before me
and to the generation after me:

My mother Malaky and my father Jacob
And to my sons Malachy, Patrick and Percival.

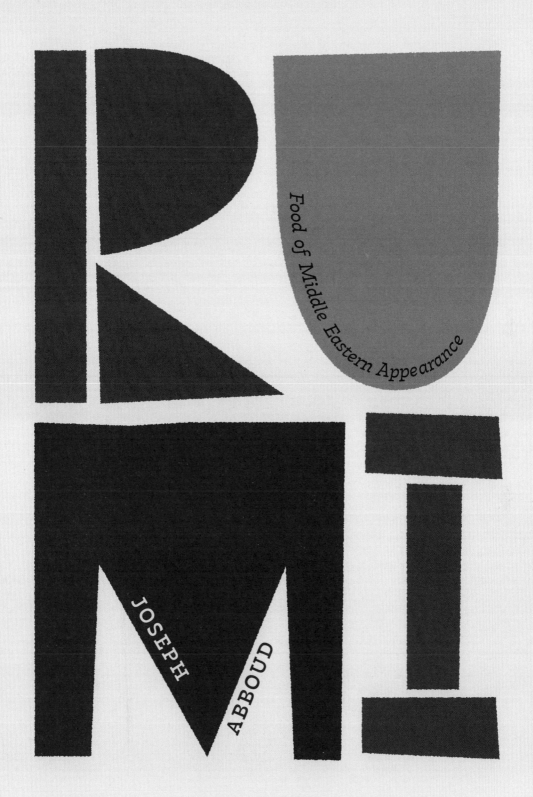

RUMI

Food of Middle Eastern Appearance

JOSEPH ABBOUD

murdoch books

Sydney | London

22

START HERE

Things I want you to know

56

SHAKS, SNACKS AND DIPS

Breakfast and other small things

FOREWORD *by Dani Valent*

Rumi had been open for a few months as 2006 ticked towards summer. The answering machine was clogged with booking requests. People lined up in the evenings, hoping to get in before the lamb meatballs ran out. For the first time in a decade of food writing, I'd heard diners rhapsodising about cauliflower, dark-fried the Rumi way and scattered with deeply caramelised onion. 'It lands on the table and you think it's burnt … but then you eat it …' was the whispered, wide-eyed word.

You'd think Joseph Abboud would be riding the sweet wave of success. But no. One afternoon I head to the restaurant to interview him for a magazine article and he is looking concerned, almost bashful. 'I'm embarrassed,' he says. 'It's overwhelming. We make food for people to eat. It's so simple. There's no way we expected this.'

Today, Brunswick East burns bright on the heatmap of Melbourne dining. It's full of little bars and funky wine shops. There's an artisan cheesemaker and fermented everything. But when Rumi opened in its first tiny corner site, there was nothing much happening – in a food sense, anyway. Indeed, Joe and his wife Nat gave newcomers directions with reference to the standout local landmark of the era: a brothel three doors down.

He wouldn't take the mantle then or now, but Joe was a trailblazer, providing a new reason to hop on the number 1 tram. Rumi's food was instantly striking for its honesty, for dishes so full of flavour they slumped with a surfeit of deliciousness, for a generosity that forged appetite even when the belly tried to say, 'enough'. Typically though, that's not how Joe spoke about his offering at the time. 'I wanted to be out of the city, out of the way, somewhere no one would see me fail,' he told me.

On this particular day in 2006, Joe was sitting under the mural depicting lines from Kahlil Gibran's prose-poem 'The Prophet'. The Arabic script brushwork was by Shahin, a friend of his dad's whose regular gig was painting the wall menus for takeaway shops. 'Shahin thought I wanted a menu too,' explained Joe. 'He asked me, "How are people going to understand what's written up there in Arabic? How will I come and change the prices if people are sitting right underneath?" We finally got through to him and then he loved it. And a while later, a customer loved it so much she got his number and had him do the same thing in her house.'

There's something emblematic in that. The vision, not always easy to sell. The penny-drop delight. And the word spreading, in this case literally. Rumi wasn't a simple proposition for everyone. Share plates were a struggle for many people in 2006. Not everyone got as far as putting the 'burnt' cauliflower in their mouth. There was the anguished case of the crying bruncher who didn't understand shakshuka. But surely, steadily, sometimes stratospherically, the project of sharing Middle Eastern culinary joy won through.

There have always been two forces at play in Joe Abboud's restaurant journey. There's the bolshie pioneer who's sure about everything, including exactly how small to chop the onions. But there's also the nervous creative, concerned that someone will see through his food's simplicity and find something lacking, refuse to be romanced by the heart, soul, heritage and utter care that truly underpins it.

One thing that's never been in doubt is the pride and commitment of Joe's parents, mother Malaky and father Jacob. They've helped him renovate – more than once. His mum has made endless staff meals and washed dishes day upon day. During the lean years of the pandemic, Jack came regularly to Rumi to peel garlic, pick herbs and trim the whiskers from prawns. In the early Rumi times, Malaky's pride extended to purchasing personalised number plates for her youngest son, immortalising the restaurant's name and its founding year. 'She bought me RUMI 06,' Joe told me that day in the restaurant. 'I said, "Mum, I'm so sorry, I can't put these on my car. You're going to have to put them on yours."' So Malaky did. For years, she drove a Ford Laser big-noting her son's restaurant. Almost two decades later she's still zipping around with the licence plates, now in a Nissan Micra. 'She cooked for us for so long,' says Joe. 'To be able to put forward our culture through these dishes is an incredible feeling. I've finally been able to give something back.'

BEGINNINGS

I came kicking and screaming to cooking. I realise it's not the typical story of a professional chef, but, truthfully, much of what I know comes from hours of research, trial and error, and persistence. Originally, I fell into cooking because I fell out of high school and told my parents that I had an apprenticeship at a French restaurant in Melbourne's CBD. It was actually a dishwashing job, but I soon fell in love with working in kitchens. I remember the first time I was sent to the cool room to grab an avocado for the chef. I didn't know what an avocado was and I could only think of an armadillo. Luckily, they look similar and both start with A.

It was at that restaurant called Oz Frog (seriously) that everything changed. I was a plain eater until the first chef I worked for there offered an apprentice some raw sea urchin. When the apprentice refused he received such a blast from the chef that when I was asked to try some myself I was so frightened that I said yes and quickly put it in my mouth. It was a revelation. Delicious and interesting. That was a key moment in my life. It unlocked something in me that I never looked back from. After that day I decided that I would try anything and everything – the silver lining to a less-than-ideal start working in kitchens.

Growing up, I had a pretty simple relationship with food, but it was a very important part of our home, and Mum cooked every meal. I was born and raised in the northern suburbs of Melbourne by my Lebanese parents, and although we were always interested in what Mum was cooking, nobody really discussed how it was made or what ingredients she chose, and I certainly didn't grow up looking over her shoulder as she cooked.

On the days Mum and Dad brought home fish and chips from the fish and chip shop they owned for us kids to eat, Mum would cook for herself and Dad because my parents didn't eat fish and chips. Sunday lunch was the most important and most anticipated meal of the week, where we all sat down together and the food was elaborate and plentiful, but it was all the incidental meals and dishes prepared on weekdays that had a lasting impact on me and are reflected in my cooking. Simple stuff, mostly: labne and za'atar sandwiches. Fried eggplant (aubergine) slices. Slow-cooked green beans. Feta and olives. Fried eggs. Most of which would be left around on the kitchen

bench for us to attack while Mum and Dad were at work all day and into the night. (Interestingly, we never got sick eating food that had been left out of the fridge all day.) Dad would take off early to their fish and chip shop and Mum would hang back a little to get us closer to being ready for school. Then, at the other end of the day, Mum would leave the shop as soon as she could to prepare dinner at home, Dad would pack down then follow on, normally getting home around 9 pm for a family dinner.

The job at Oz Frog turned out to be a baptism of fire. Some weeks we weren't being paid anything, and others only $50, so really, I should have seen it coming – even at the age of 16 – when a supplier came in looking for money and the chef (who was also the owner) told him that the owner never comes in and he was just the chef. One day I arrived at the restaurant to find chains on the door. The landlord had locked the owner out for unpaid rent.

This was Melbourne in the early nineties, and with the recession and a high unemployment rate there weren't many jobs around in general, let alone for apprentice chefs. There weren't even many restaurants, so it turned out to be a real challenge to find an apprenticeship. I gave up hope after a while, realising that I just needed a job. Any job. This was the ethos that I was brought up with; as much as getting an education was valued, work gave you ultimate power. So long as you had a job and knew how to work you would be okay. And once you had a job you worked and saved as hard as you could. This led to me selling discounted cards door to door. I was not very good at it despite the fact that so many early Lebanese migrants to Australia were hawkers.

But the pull of the kitchen was still strong, so I restarted my search for an apprenticeship. Eventually I landed a job in a dysfunctional suburban pub kitchen but, pretty quickly, the chef convinced me that I would have to get out of there if I wanted to learn anything. He was right. After all, deep-frying frozen potato wedges and scraping mould off 20-litre buckets of risotto was not an ideal starting point.

The first three years of my apprenticeship were a slow climb from the pub to a groovy cafe to an edgy pizzeria until, one day, I ate at a fine dining restaurant for the first time in my life: Jacques Reymond in Melbourne. I discovered that this cooking caper was something else. Even though high-end dining was foreign to me, I thought that I had to get some experience of it if I was ever going to make progress in my cooking career. After a number of unsuccessful trials with Jacques, I gave up, but could not forget the fresh smell of the cool room, the care that was taken in the kitchen, the detail of the dishes and the intensity of the work.

I knew little about the hospitality industry, nor who I should talk to. I took the advice of the chef of one of my cooking school

"I was born and raised in the northern suburbs of Melbourne and although we were always interested in what mum was cooking, nobody really discussed how it was made or what ingredients she chose."

friends (Freddy; we remain friends to this day) to check out a place called Est Est Est. The advice was to hassle them until they let me in the door. Hassle I did. The first time I knocked on the door – some time in November 1997 – chef Donovan Cooke answered, squinting into the sun, and asked in a less-than-friendly manner what I wanted. I told him I wanted to work there, and he pretty much told me to piss off and come back in January. So, I did. He was even less impressed the second time I showed up, but took pity on me and said I could come in for a trial. By this time, I had been cooking for around three years and thought I knew a bit about it – working at Est Est Est showed me how little I really knew. It completely blew me away. The trial shift started at 9 am with peeling tomatoes, a somewhat simple preparation that should have been familiar, but these guys quickly had me wondering if there was some special tomato peeler I didn't know about.

Music in the Est Est Est kitchen blared at a volume that removed any possibility for conversation. It heightened anxiety and seemed to reverberate at a level you might associate with warfare. I wonder if they were trying to get our hearts racing faster to match the music. As the son of Lebanese parents, my sheltered outer-suburban ears had never heard Led Zeppelin, Radiohead, Van Morrison. Everything was a revelation. I had never seen such attention to detail. Little did I know that other than a strictly enforced one-hour break for a staff meal (which was better than anything I'd ever tasted before) this pace would continue until about midnight. Surely this wasn't normal. Surely the cleaners would be in soon. We'd been working since 9 am. I was so naive. When I was handed the scrubbing pad to bring the target top stove back to bare metal, I realised there weren't any cleaners – this was a normal day. Every day.

During this madness and superhuman/inhumane activity, I would be given little scraps of food to taste, including the most incredible desserts from Philippa Sibley that were so revelatory that the hook was well and truly in. It was now a matter of whether or not Donovan would throw me back in the water or keep me. He said I could keep coming back as long as I understood that I would have to keep on trialling until he thought I could cut it. Before my next trial, I parked my car around the corner 15 minutes before my shift and tried to replicate the motivational music scenes of Sylvester Stallone in *Rocky*. I blasted the music that I knew and loved: Prince; the NPG (a band started by Prince), and added a few motivational roars at the top of my lungs before making my way to the kitchen door. Again and again, I was met by the cold hard reality of chefs who were only interested in surviving the day and mastering their craft at what I soon learned was considered one of the best restaurants in the country. I needed something more than Prince to get me through this. Eventually, I secured a job there and saw out an entire year – the most demoralising, humiliating, enriching and motivating experience of my life.

A young Josh Emett was working there at that time. Among the sometimes incredibly harsh lessons I learned from him was that I had to leave my pride at the door. There was no room for my thoughts or feelings. Without his tough teachings and support I don't think I would have lasted a month, let alone a year. One particular episode sticks out. It was one of many times that the pace and intensity beat me. I escaped to the back laneway and sobbed uncontrollably. Josh came out and stood beside me. No words of solace, just a presence. There was nothing he could say. There was no changing the situation. This is what I had signed up for. He also taught me to make gnocchi and pick spinach like I was possessed. I completed the final year of my apprenticeship at Est Est Est.

I decided that I didn't have the stamina or will to live my working life at that pace, so it was time to move on. I happily took a job at Circa with renowned chef Michael Lambie. During the 18 months that I worked there I heard talk of a Lebanese chef named Greg Malouf. He was cooking contemporary fine dining food influenced by Lebanese and broader Middle Eastern flavours. At that point, I hadn't even considered taking my cooking in that direction, but I was presented with an opportunity to work at a special event with Greg and I jumped at the chance.

While at Circa I saved for the trip of a lifetime – an idea that had slowly been bubbling away in my mind. Finally, in February 2001, I bought a one-way ticket to Hong Kong and headed into the unknown. I backpacked along the old Silk Road for almost a year. It was a formative journey – particularly my time in the Middle East – which would have the greatest impact on my cooking and, of course, this book. I could recount many stories here, like how I slept on the sand dunes of the Taklamakan Desert in far-west China where they bury their grapevines in the sand in winter because it gets so cold, or how I shared a plate of the tiniest okra with the locals in the mountains of Pakistan's Karakoram Highway. I could tell you how I shared a meal with a family (who spoke not a word of English) in their home in Iran, or the time I ate so much bread in Turkey I nearly ended up in hospital. I could tell you about the best shawarma I've ever eaten that made me violently ill while in Damascus. I could share with you the deep sense of comfort I felt sitting on a low table and stools in my grandparents' tiny kitchen in the north of Lebanon, eating a pan of eggs, fresh labne and home-grown cured green olives with my grandfather. And I could go on, with stories like the time I left my hostel in the early morning in Palermo, Sicily to discover a nonna frying arancini in a giant cauldron of oil on the side of the path to the market. But this is not a travel journal. It's just a little context.

> "I knew what Middle Eastern food should taste like. The first time I made tabbouleh it was delicious, simply because I knew what it looked like and how it was supposed to taste."

In Positano, Italy, during one of my rare phone calls home, my parents told me that they'd heard from the owner of a small restaurant in Kilmore in regional Victoria. He was wondering if I'd like to try it out as a venue for my first restaurant. Mum and Dad, knowing my entrepreneurial tendencies, thought it was a great idea. They also thought that just coming home might be a great idea too.

I knew little about the area. It was a fairly conservative country town and I tried to reflect that in my menu. I hadn't considered just how conservative it was, and that the locals didn't tend to eat out in fancy restaurants. I did, however, get to meet some interesting customers, particularly some winemakers in the area who started as regulars and eventually became friends. A small following of appreciative customers didn't pay the bills though, and eventually I decided to pull the plug, go back to the drawing board and explore the idea of working with Greg Malouf at MoMo restaurant.

Because I had come from a cooking background of hard graft and aggression with an ego to match, and because MoMo was a gentler place, I had a complex relationship with Greg and the restaurant. I ended up doing two short stints there, the second of which was working with Kurt Sampson who taught me much about breaking away from the traditional – and to calm down a little. The food that Greg created confirmed for me that it was food of Middle Eastern appearance that I wanted to cook. Greg showed me that the flavours of our heritage could be enhanced and refreshed by our European training, and Kurt pointed me towards exciting and unusual Middle Eastern food marriages.

After MoMo I did another stint working with Donovan Cooke and Philippa Sibley at Ondine restaurant in Melbourne's CBD. Now that I was no longer an apprentice regularly being yelled at, at Ondine I was able to appreciate the skill, knowledge and quest for perfection that drove Donovan. It was also at Ondine that I realised I needed to learn the European palate. Although I hadn't had much experience cooking Lebanese food (fat chance of Mum letting me into the kitchen; she still warns me to be careful with a knife), I knew what Middle Eastern food should taste like. The first time I made tabbouleh it was delicious, simply because I knew what it should look like and how it was supposed to taste. When Ondine closed I knew it was time to head in my own direction. I didn't have the aspiration or commitment of a young chef wanting to reach 'the top' of haute cuisine – instead, it was time to go back to my roots.

Joseph Abboud

OF MIDDLE EASTERN APPEARANCE

On September 11, 2001, when those devastating attacks occurred in New York, I was in Aleppo, Syria. I came home for Christmas, worrying about how I would get through the airport with passport stamps from Pakistan, Iran, Turkey (twice), Syria (twice) and Lebanon.

Re-entering Australia was not a problem for me, but 9/11 was certainly a turning point for Arab Australians. Arabs (a loose term in itself) became the target of some nasty attacks, but even more worrying was the frequent labelling of people 'of Middle Eastern appearance'. Any time someone did something wrong we waited to find out if they were 'of Middle Eastern appearance' so that we could hang our heads in shame. I actually like the term, hence the subtitle of this book; my concern is more around how and when these words are used. When someone 'of Anglo appearance' commits a crime, there is no mention of what they look like. In the brainstorming days before we opened Rumi, my mother-in-law, Mem, suggested that we describe my food as 'of Middle Eastern appearance'. This may have gone some way towards helping realign the pejorative way that the description was being used, but I didn't have the courage to follow through with her suggestion. It was just too soon.

I tried to write this book excluding the politics, but soon came to realise that one of the driving factors behind Rumi's birth as a restaurant was the opportunity to provide a counterbalance to the narrative that was so prevalent. My use of the expression in the title of this book was to draw attention to the fact that the much-loved poet-philosopher Rumi; the author of 'The Prophet', Kahlil Gibran, whose poetry adorns the walls; Steve Bracks, former Victorian Premier; Zaha Hadid, famed international architect; actor Omar Sharif; model Gigi Hadid; Jacques Nasser, former Ford CEO, and even Jesus, were all 'of Middle Eastern appearance'.

I am of Middle Eastern appearance. As is my food.

> "I am of Middle Eastern appearance. As is my food."

MIDDLE EASTERN FOOD, THIS BOOK, AND HOW TO USE IT

Cooking actually doesn't come easily to me. Consequently, I have always found it easy to teach people what I have learned because I break it down simply in a way that even I would understand. You'll find some Q&As at the end of some recipes – these are the sorts of questions I would be likely to ask, and that would stop me from giving the recipe a go, so I hope my answers are helpful to you too. I'm also hoping that this gives you the confidence to mess around with the recipes and make them work for you. Remember, you're the one who will be eating them. Most recipes aren't heavily affected by a missing ingredient. For example, if you really don't like a lot of garlic (you poor thing), you can reduce or omit it from most recipes, or perhaps you don't like eggplant (aubergine) – try the recipe with zucchini (courgette) or pumpkin (squash) instead. If you don't like chickpeas but you want to make hummus, try my Almond taratoor (page 85).

When preparing Middle Eastern food, you don't need any specialist equipment or utensils, just some big bowls for mixing salads, a deep-fryer, a food processor and, if you really want to have some fun, a charcoal grill. You could add a mortar and pestle or spice grinder to the list too. None of these are unique to Middle Eastern food – you probably have them already. The same applies to the majority of ingredients used in Middle Eastern food – you probably already cook with most of them, but there are a handful of non-perishable staples that you could add to your pantry to make the cooking a little easier. Ingredients such as sumac, allspice, tahini and pomegranate molasses come to mind. Gentle spices such as cinnamon, nutmeg and cloves that are often used for sweet dishes in European cooking find their way into seasoning vegetable braises or meat for the grill. This accessibility to ingredients means that once you have prepared some of the recipes in the first chapter of this book, you will find that a comforting roast (served with Muhammara, page 37), weeknight barbecued meat (brushed with Toum, page 34, and za'atar) or your next festivity (with a spread of vegetable salads) can be given a Middle Eastern boost quite easily.

Middle Eastern food is great for entertaining as many dishes can be partly or fully prepared in advance, reducing the

> "You are not trying to impress your mother-in-law with age-old recipes that can't be deviated from, so have some fun and feel free to mix it up a little."

workload when your guests are around. You are not trying to impress your mother-in-law with age-old recipes that can't be deviated from, so have some fun and feel free to mix it up.

There can be a mystique around spices, but the truth is you don't need to 'understand' them. We don't need to 'understand' onions. We just use them. Sure, if you want to become dedicated to your craft, you may want to dig a little deeper into different flavour combinations and uses, but if you're reading this book, something tells me you're just looking for something satisfying to cook and eat. Of course, there is an undeniable joy in buying whole spices and grinding them yourself, but it's also really fine to buy them already ground. Mum has been doing it for years. I don't think she 'knows' the first thing about spices, but if you can cook as well as she can, you're doing pretty well. Fresh spices are unquestionably best, but they can be stored for months. I know this is not recommended, but wars were fought over spices, so I'd prefer you don't throw them away because they've been sitting around for a while.

The first chapter covers many recipes that will not only make cooking out of the rest of the book easier, but you'll find ways to use them in your everyday food preparation. For example, you may find yourself using a spoonful of Toum (page 34) in the next pasta you make, or rubbing Advieh (page 24) on a roast chicken. You'll be able to reach into your fridge for some fried almonds (page 41) to add to your next salad, or even dress your grilled asparagus with Taratoor (page 42). The recipes in this section all make more than you'll need for any one recipe, the idea being that you will have plenty of each on standby to give a dish some Middle Eastern flair.

The chapters that follow include many recipes that have become Rumi classics over the years – many that I would not take off the menu for fear of a revolt. I share these with a little trepidation, not because they are guarded secrets, but because their simplicity may surprise you. One of the most loved dishes at Rumi is the slow-cooked lamb shoulder (page 128), yet it is one of the easiest in this book. Time, a few ingredients and a little love is all you need.

Then there are other recipes that are a little less well defined. Some from past menus and some that take some creative licence. Although I'm not one to insist that traditional is better, I do think that if it is not as good or better than the original, then innovation for its own sake is vain, and pointless.

Being raised Lebanese gave me a head start in understanding the essence of the cuisine, but I've never been shy to venture off the beaten track. I've loved the hours sifting through Turkish, Persian and Lebanese grocery stores asking the shopkeepers about the context of each ingredient before taking them back to the kitchen to work with. Ingredients such as Salça, a Turkish red pepper paste that has found its way into butter and has limitless applications, or Persian pickled grapes that became a dressing for barbecued fish and meats. I was pleasantly surprised to learn that these unripe grapes are also used to make hossrom (verjuice), which is an alternative to lemon throughout the Middle East.

Once you have played with my recipes and have experimented with your own changes to them, you are likely to want to keep going. If you are after the great authority on Middle Eastern food, you can't go past Claudia Roden's *The New Book of Middle Eastern Food*. Claudia's work has become so well absorbed into chefs' Middle Eastern recipes that its hard to know where her recipes end and others' begin. Her work has been a consistent source of inspiration for me. In a recent interview, she articulated perfectly how I feel about my own food and this book. Of her cookbooks, she said: 'My strengths limit my dish to a simplicity that I am happy with. Also, that my readers would be happy with.'

TABBOULEH WITHOUT TOMATOES
On Authenticity in Food

What do you mean my food isn't Lebanese? Well, what makes food Lebanese? The chef, the creator? The ingredients? Are they indigenous? And what about with music? Is it the singer? The song? The instruments? The record company? So, I'm told my fattoush isn't Lebanese because it contains peas and asparagus among other 'alien' things. Traditional? Maybe not, but who would argue that the music of Fairuz isn't Lebanese? Fairuz sings classical Arabic to a Western music orchestra. Traditional?

I've heard it said that Hamed Sinno of Mashrou' Leila isn't even singing Arabic half the time. I know that it may not be traditional to slur your speech while singing in Arabic, but you try to tell Mashrou' Leila that they aren't Lebanese artists ... so why can't I put dill and almonds in my fava beans?

I always emphasise the fact that tomatoes have only been in Lebanon for about 300 years. At some point some nutter would have had to add tomatoes to their parsley and burghul to make an 'inauthentic' tabbouleh. We would never accept a tabbouleh without tomatoes now. The same goes for the keyboard in Lebanese music. Not sure how long it's been around but I can bet the first time someone whipped out a keyboard during a jam session at EMI, it wasn't met with ease. So I'm sorry, this time we aren't going to mash the barbecued eggplants (aubergines).

Is the reluctance to accept new styles of food and music as part of our own culture a reflection of people struggling to evolve? Where do we start?

A version of this piece was originally published in The Carton, *a Beirut-based magazine on Lebanese food culture and the Middle East.*

HERE

These recipes are the pillars of many of the dishes in the following chapters, and starting here, with some spice mixes, flavoured butters, or key ingredients like Toum (page 34) and Labne (page 31), will immediately set you on the path to deliciousness. Having a few of these on hand will make cooking the recipes in this book a breeze.

ADVIEH

·All recipes pictured on page 27–28

Advieh is Iran's version of India's garam masala or Morocco's ras el hanout.
It's a spice mix that differs from place to place depending on the use and region.
It contains many of the usual suspects, such as cumin, cinnamon and nutmeg,
as well as the dried rose and dried lime that are more unique to Persian cuisine.
I don't know where this recipe began, but I have made adjustments along the
way to make it my own. It is used in our meatballs (see page 130) and on our
slow-roasted lamb shoulder (see page 128) but occasionally it finds its way into a
Khoresht (Persian curry; see page 156) or as a marinade for barbecued fish.

Mix all the ingredients well and store in an airtight jar or container
for 3–6 months.

Note
*Of course, best practice would be to buy all the ingredients whole and
grind them yourself, but it's okay to buy them already ground. If there
is any one ingredient that I would advise grinding yourself, it would be
the dried limes. When you buy them already ground, their powder is
bitter because they are ground with the seeds. If you are going to the
effort of grinding them yourself, cut them in half and remove the seeds
before crushing and grinding.*

Q. What is golpar powder?
*A. Golpar is a mysterious ingredient that has a mild curry-like flavour.
I have found it listed as anything from wild parsley to angelica. I don't
believe it is actually either of those. You'll have to buy it from Persian
or Afghan grocers.*

Makes 250 g (9 oz)

10 g (¼ oz) dried rose powder
15 g (½ oz) golpar powder
15 g (½ oz) ground turmeric
15 g (½ oz) ground black
  peppercorns
50 g (1¾ oz) ground cinnamon
30 g (1 oz) ground nutmeg
15 g (½ oz) ground cardamom
50 g (1¾ oz) ground cumin
35 g (1¼ oz) ground coriander
20 g (¾ oz) dried lime powder

BAHARAT

This is a very simple soft spice house mix that can be used to enhance literally
anything from barbecue to tabbouleh.

Mix all the ingredients well and store in an airtight jar or
container for 3–6 months.

Note
*You could add 15 g (½ oz) each of ground cumin and coriander to make
Lebanese 7 spice.*
  *Feel free to buy whole spices and grind them yourself, but pre-ground
spices work just as well and, chances are, you probably already have some
of them in your cupboard.*

Makes 65 g (2½ oz)

20 g (¾ oz) ground cinnamon
10 g (¼ oz) ground allspice
15 g (½ oz) ground nutmeg
5 g (⅛ oz) ground cloves
15 g (½ oz) ground black
  peppercorns

SPICED SALTS

Spiced salts are easy to make and store. They give roasted or barbecued meats, seafoods or vegetables a little kick just before serving. Store in airtight containers in your pantry for 3–6 months.

Makes 100 g (3½ oz)

Fennel salt
20 g (¾ oz) fennel seeds
80 g (2¾ oz) salt flakes

Advieh salt
10 g (¼ oz) Advieh
  (see opposite)
90 g (3¼ oz) salt flakes

FOR THE FENNEL SALT
Lightly toast the fennel seeds over a medium heat in a small dry frying pan. The seeds can be left whole, crushed or a combination of both.
  Mix with the salt.

FOR THE ADVIEH SALT
Mix the advieh and salt together.

DUKKAH

Correctly pronounced 'dou'a', dukkah basically means smashed, and it seems to go well on everything from roasted vegetables to ice cream. The genesis of this particular recipe is Claudia Roden's book, The New Book of Middle Eastern Food. *I made the addition of nigella seeds. You can use macadamia nuts instead of the hazelnuts here for an Australian accent.*

Makes 175 g (6 oz)

15 g (½ oz) nigella seeds
25 g (1 oz) salt flakes
50 g (⅓ cup) sesame seeds,
  toasted
50 g (1¾ oz) hazelnuts, roasted
  and peeled
25 g (1 oz) coriander seeds,
  toasted
25 g (1 oz) cumin seeds, toasted

In a bowl, place the nigella seeds, salt flakes and sesame seeds.
  Lightly crush the hazelnuts in a mortar and pestle (I like to leave them a bit chunky). Add to the bowl.
  Blend the coriander and cumin seeds in a spice grinder until fine. I like to take some of the seeds out before they get too fine. Add to the bowl and mix.
  Store in an airtight container in the fridge for up to 3 months.

Clockwise from top:
Advieh (page 24),
Baharat (page 24),
Advieh salt (page 25),
Dukkah (page 25),
Fennel salt (page 25)

SALÇA BUTTER

Turkish Salça is a red paste similar in appearance to tomato paste, but made from dried capsicum (pepper). Salça butter is simply a combination of butter and Salça that, when cooked together, creates a complex flavour rich in umami.

Melt the butter in a small saucepan over a medium heat.

Whisk in the Salça and cook over a low heat for about an hour, stirring occasionally.

The butter should smell a little cheesy when it is ready. Remove from the heat and allow it to cool completely.

Once cool, transfer the butter to a container and seal. Stir the butter before it sets completely as the Salça will sink. This butter will keep in the fridge for up to 3 months.

Makes 360 g (12¾ oz)

300 g (10½ oz) salted butter
60 g (2¼ oz) Salça (red pepper paste)

MINT BUTTER

I love the combination of burnt butter and yoghurt. The mint gives this butter a beautiful aroma that perfectly complements the nutty flavour.

Melt the butter in a small saucepan over a medium heat, then reduce the heat to low and cook for about 10 minutes until the butter is brown and smells nutty.

Whisk in the dried mint. Remove from the heat and allow it to cool completely.

Once cool, transfer the butter to a container and seal. You will need to stir the butter before it sets completely as the dried mint will sink. This butter will keep in the fridge for up to 3 months.

Makes 300 g (10½ oz)

300 g (10½ oz) salted butter
2 tablespoons dried mint

SEKANJABIN

This sweet-and-sour syrup is used in Iran as a cordial and for dipping cos leaves into. I highly recommend both, as well as the Lamb shoulder (page 128), Sweet-and-sour dressing (page 47) and Cos and herb salad (page 115), which also use this syrup.

Bring the sugar, vinegar and 150 ml (5 fl oz) of water to the boil in a saucepan and cook until it reduces by one-third.

Add the mint, remove from the heat and leave to cool so the flavour can infuse.

Makes 400 g (14 oz)

500 g (1 lb 2 oz) raw sugar
25 ml (¾ fl oz) white wine vinegar
¼ bunch of mint, roughly chopped

YOGHURT

·All recipes pictured on page 32–33

Making yoghurt will give you great bang for your buck. With very little effort you can turn milk – even out-of-date milk – into something beautiful. It's as simple as bringing milk to the boil, letting it cool to a certain point, adding some yoghurt as a starter, giving it a blessing (or not, if you're an atheist), then keeping it warm for about eight hours.

We make about 30 litres of yoghurt every day at Rumi and I never get sick of opening up the bucket of what was milk and seeing that it has become yoghurt. Yoghurt is only sweet if you add a sweetener. Left alone, it is creamy and slightly sour. Sometimes Greek.

MUM'S METHOD

Lightly brush the inside of a pot with the oil – this will stop the milk sticking to the bottom of the pan when it boils. Add enough cold water to just coat the bottom of the pot, then pour in the milk.

Bring the milk to the boil over a medium heat, then tip it into a container of your choice (we use old yoghurt buckets at Rumi) and allow to cool.

When the milk has cooled enough for you to comfortably hold your pinky finger in it for a count of 20 (about 45°C/113°F), it's ready to add the yoghurt and gently stir.

Pop on a lid, wrap the container in a blanket and bless (or not), then leave to cool very slowly. You could put the wrapped pot in an esky or cool box to ensure slow cooling.

After 8 hours of cooling, place the container in the fridge for a further 6–8 hours.

SUGGESTED WORKFLOW

Heat milk to boiling point while watching Arabic news, keeping one eye on the stove so the milk doesn't boil over.

Allow to cool while watching dubbed Turkish soap operas; add yoghurt culture.

Wrap and leave while you sleep.

Refrigerate and leave while you are at work.

Makes 2 kg (4 lb 8 oz)

neutral-flavoured oil, such as canola oil, for greasing

2 litres (8 cups) full-cream milk

1 tablespoon natural yoghurt (see Note)

Note
You must start with real live natural yoghurt from the shops or ask a friend who makes their own yoghurt for some culture.

Watch the milk carefully while it is coming to the boil; the second you turn around it will erupt like a volcano.

It's very important that the milk comes to the boil because it denatures the whey proteins, which allows it to set better (plus my dad says you should and he's a great backseat cook who can barely cook an egg).

LABNE

Please do not buy labne. Even if you don't make your own yoghurt, making your own labne is a must; it's super super easy. You literally salt some yoghurt then strain through muslin or cheesecloth. Labne can be the base for many condiments and sauces but is really a treat on its own.

Makes 400 g (14 oz)

1 kg (2 lb 4 oz) natural
  yoghurt
2 teaspoons salt

Note
You can go old school and tip the yoghurt into a cloth money bag (if these things still exist) as my mum used to and hang the bag of yoghurt over the sink to drain. When we first opened Rumi we used to use pillowcases!

A lot of liquid (whey) will drain away, mostly in the first few hours. Be sure to check the container underneath so you don't end up with an overflowing mess. The whey is an incredibly satisfying thirst quencher, especially on a hot day.

Line a strainer with some cheesecloth, ensuring that you leave some cloth hanging over the edges.

Place the yoghurt in a bowl and whisk in the salt. Transfer to the lined strainer and suspend the strainer over a bucket or bowl to catch the whey.

The labne will be ready in 12–48 hours depending on how thick you like it – it's usually ready when it's about the texture of cream cheese. You can refrigerate it for this period if you like, but Mum always leaves hers out.

Your labne will keep in an airtight container in the fridge for up to 2 weeks.

TAHINI YOGHURT

This yoghurt is a gateway drug to an all-tahini sauce (see page 42). If you just like a little tahini, then the creaminess and acidity of the yoghurt really works to balance it out.

Makes 500 g (1 lb 2 oz)

125 g (4½ oz) tahini
½ tablespoon Toum (page 34)
300 g (10½ oz) natural
  yoghurt
75 ml (⅓ cup) lemon juice
1 teaspoon salt

Add all the ingredients to a mixing bowl and whisk until combined and smooth. Season to taste with salt, then transfer to a bottle or jars and store in the fridge for up to 1 week.

Clockwise from top: Yoghurt (page 30), Labne (page 31), Tahini yoghurt (page 31)

TOUM

The problem with toum is that you'll find yourself using it everywhere, and everything you make ends up 'needing toum'. If you're not sure what toum is, it is the Arabic word for garlic as well as the paste that is a combination of garlic, oil, salt and lemon – almost like a thick garlic mayonnaise without egg.

Blitz the whole garlic cloves with the salt in a food processor for 20–30 seconds.

Slowly add half the oil, as you would for mayonnaise, ensuring the mix does not split. This should take about 2 minutes.

Add half the lemon juice, then most of the remaining oil. This can be added a little faster. Add the remaining lemon juice, then the last of the oil.

You can add a little iced water to make the toum fluffy, white and a little softer, if you like.

Store in an airtight container in the fridge for up to 2 weeks.

Note
Weigh your ingredients and refrigerate for a few hours until cold before making your toum. Cool the blade of your blender too if that's an option. Keeping everything cold like this will prevent your toum from splitting.
If your garlic is a little old and has a green shoot in the centre, split the clove and pick out the green shoot, as it can add an unwelcome bitterness to your toum.

Makes 600 g (1 lb 5 oz)

150 g (5½ oz) garlic cloves, peeled
8 g (¼ oz) salt
500 ml (2 cups) canola oil
70 ml (2¼ fl oz) lemon juice
iced water (optional)

SOUSED ONIONS

· Recipe pictured on page 38

These are quick pickled onions that make a great addition to any salad, such as the Summer and Spring fattoush recipes on pages 118 and 121.

Place the sliced onions in a bowl and toss with the salt. Leave to stand for a couple of hours.

Transfer to a jar or container and cover with the vinegar, then seal and refrigerate.

The onions will be ready to use the following day and will keep in the fridge for 1 month.

Note
The shape and thickness of the onions doesn't matter too much, so don't get hung up on that part.

Makes 300 g (10½ oz)

2 red onions, sliced into crescents 2 mm (¹⁄₁₆ in) thick
2 teaspoons salt
250 ml (1 cup) red wine vinegar

Q. I don't have any red wine vinegar, can I use another type?
A. Yes, you can. The red wine vinegar accentuates the red colour, but it isn't essential.

Harissa

Recipe pictured on page 38

Harissa is a North African chilli paste. I don't normally cook from North African cuisines, but harissa has made its way into our kitchen nonetheless. This doctored version is more of a sauce than the traditional paste. It gives a fragrant fiery hit to your condiment selection, yet still works if you tone down the chilli content.

Makes 450 g (1 lb)

2 large red capsicums (peppers) or 300 g (10½ oz) roasted and peeled weight

50 g (1¾ oz) long red chilli, deseeded and roughly chopped

1 teaspoon salt

10 g (¼ oz) coriander seeds, toasted and ground

10 g (¼ oz) cumin seeds, toasted and ground

1½ tablespoons Toum (page 34) or 3 garlic cloves, crushed

150 ml (5 fl oz) vegetable oil

Start by charring the capsicums over an open flame or gas barbecue. The skin should be black all over, which will make peeling them easier. Set aside in a colander to drain and cool. Once the capsicums are cool enough to handle, rub off the charred skins. Remove the stem and split the capsicum open to remove its seeds. Cut the flesh into bite-sized pieces to assist with blending.

Place the chilli, salt, spices and toum in a food processor and blend until smooth.

Add a few tablespoons of the oil to help form a paste that will blend evenly, stopping occasionally to scrape down the sides. Add the capsicum then blend until smooth.

Now you can add the remaining oil slowly, as you would for toum or mayonnaise, so it combines with the capsicum. This should take about 1 minute.

Store in an airtight container in the fridge for up to 2 weeks.

CRISPY ONIONS

Makes 35 g (½ cup)

1 small onion

500 ml (2 cups) oil, for deep-frying (see page 49)

salt, to taste

Slice the onion very thinly into rings – as thin as you can get them – using something like a mandolin for consistency. Rinse in a bowl of cold water, then drain and spread on some paper towel to dry.

Heat the oil in a saucepan or deep-fryer until it reaches 160°C (315°F) on a cooking thermometer.

Sprinkle the onion into the hot oil and fry until light brown (it will continue to colour as it cools). Remove and spread on some paper towel to drain. Sprinkle with salt immediately.

MUHAMMARA

· Recipe pictured on page 38

Muhammara has come and gone from our repertoire over the years, and has appeared on everything from baked fish to barbecued beetroot (beet). The sweet–sour pomegranate molasses is great with the red capsicums (peppers). You can leave out the walnuts if you have a nut allergy and this recipe will still give you joy.

Makes 500 g (1 lb 2 oz)

2 large red capsicums (peppers), or 280 g (10 oz) drained tinned roasted capsicum

120 g (4¼ oz) walnuts

50 g (1¾ oz) pomegranate molasses

2 teaspoons ground cumin

1 teaspoon Turkish chilli powder

1 teaspoon salt

120 ml (½ cup) extra-virgin olive oil

Start by charring the capsicums over an open flame or gas barbecue. The skin should be black all over, which will make peeling them easier. Set aside in a colander to drain and cool. Once the capsicums are cool enough to handle, rub off the charred skins. Remove the stem and split the capsicum open to remove its seeds. Cut the flesh into bite-sized pieces to assist with blending.

In a blender or food processor, pulse the walnuts until they have a coarse consistency, something akin to granola. Remove half and add to a mixing bowl. I do this because I like the idea of some crunch left in the mix, but I also like the fine walnuts to be one with the other ingredients. Continue to blend the remaining walnuts until they resemble almond meal.

Add the capsicum and remaining ingredients, except for the oil, in the food processor and blend until smooth, stopping occasionally to scrape down the sides. Now you can add the oil slowly, so it combines with the capsicum. Transfer to the bowl with the coarse walnuts and combine well. I like to finish with a tablespoon of water, which makes it look creamier and more combined.

Store in an airtight container in the fridge for up to 2 weeks.

Note
If you are having a charcoal barbecue, try roasting your capsicums after you've finished cooking but while the coals are still glowing. This gives an extra depth of flavour to the finished dish.

You can extend this recipe by adding some water and adjusting the seasoning to turn it into more of a sauce, which is great on barbecued vegetables and meats. In this case, I would blend all the walnuts until smooth.

Top to bottom:
Harissa (page 36),
Muhammara
(page 37), Soused
onions (page 34)

FRIED NUTS

One of the most beautiful features of Middle Eastern cooking is the use of nuts. Europe has pork, the Middle East has nuts. They provide the crunch and contrast that many chefs look for when creating a dish. Pine nuts, almonds, pistachios and walnuts are most commonly used for savoury dishes. Traditionally, nuts are toasted in oil or butter as the dish is being prepared, but for the purpose of my recipes, I toast the nuts then store them to have on hand when I need them. There's a special pleasure in opening your fridge to see a container of golden toasted nuts looking back at you, volunteering itself to join your meal.

Unlike many other cuisines, which use lightly toasted nuts, in Middle Eastern cooking, you fry the nuts. The most common nuts you will need to fry for my recipes are pine nuts, pistachios and almonds. Below is an example of quantities and how to fry them, but you can increase the amount of oil as you increase the amount of nuts. If you have a deep-fryer, you can just drop the nuts directly into the fryer basket, but only if the mesh is fine enough to hold them. (You don't want to be fishing around the bottom of a deep-fryer for your precious pine nuts that are quickly burning.)

If you are using a saucepan, you will need to prepare a second saucepan or bowl containing a strainer to drain the oil immediately after cooking the nuts.

Makes 95 g (1 cup)

500 ml (2 cups) vegetable oil, for deep-frying (see page 49)
95 g (1 cup) flaked almonds, pistachios or pine nuts

Heat the oil in a saucepan over a medium–high heat. You'll know it's hot enough when a couple of almonds dropped into the oil sizzle gently. Place the rest of the almonds into the hot oil. This will temporarily reduce the temperature of the oil, but stir occasionally and the temperature will come back up and the almonds will start to sizzle. Turn the heat down to low and stir more frequently until the nuts are light brown.

Because the nuts will continue to cook even after you take them out of the oil, quickly drain them in a strainer, allowing any excess oil to drain away. They will smell fantastic but don't be tempted to taste them straight away, as they will be VERY hot.

Spread the nuts on a plate or tray lined with paper towel and allow to cool before storing in a sealed container in the fridge for up to 3 months.

Note
The oil can also be reused once or twice at a later date. Once cooled, pour it into a container, seal with the lid and refrigerate.
   I recommend storing your nuts in the fridge before and after toasting them. They just keep better that way.

TaRaTOOR

One-minute tahini sauce

·All recipes pictured on page 44

Tahini sauce, correctly called 'taratoor', is a versatile sauce that is traditionally used on anything from falafel to baked fish. I find myself reaching for it time and time again when looking for a creamy addition to many dishes, especially if they are vegan. We often have guests double-checking that the dishes with tahini in them are, in fact, vegan due to the richness that comes from the taratoor.

Place all the ingredients in a jar or container, in the order in which they're listed, with 150 ml (5 fl oz) water. Seal with a tight-fitting lid and shake, shake, shake!

The sauce may be very thick depending on the tahini, but it can be easily adjusted with a touch of water. You want it to be the consistency of single (pure) cream. This sauce will also thicken after refrigeration. Just add a little water to adjust the consistency. Store in an airtight container in the fridge for up to 2 weeks.

Makes 400 ml (14 fl oz)

80 ml (⅓ cup) lemon juice

2 tablespoons verjuice

10 g (¼ oz) garlic, crushed to a fine paste, or 15 g (½ oz) Toum (page 34)

8 g (¼ oz) salt

1 tablespoon extra-virgin olive oil

200 g (7 oz) tahini

Green taratoor

Use the Taratoor to make this variation, which is beautiful to look at and has the addition of loads of fresh herbs that go so well with the rich tahini.

Makes 250 ml (1 cup)

½ bunch of flat-leaf parsley leaves
½ bunch of coriander (cilantro), trimmed of the roots
½ bunch of dill
1 long green chilli, deseeded
1 teaspoon Toum (page 34)
200 ml (7 fl oz) Taratoor (see opposite)
salt, to taste

Wash and roughly chop the herbs and chilli. Add to a food processor or blender with the toum and one-quarter of the taratoor and blend until the herbs are finely chopped. Add the remaining taratoor and blend gently to combine. You may also want to add salt, to taste.

Store in an airtight container in the fridge for up to 1 week.

Red taratoor

This is a rich variation of Taratoor that has that extra umami from the Salça. Use anywhere that you would use regular taratoor.

Makes 250 ml (1 cup)

200 ml (7 fl oz) Taratoor (see opposite)
70 g (2½ oz) Salça (red pepper paste)

Combine the taratoor and Salça in a bowl and whisk thoroughly, or you could use a blender.

Store in an airtight container in the fridge for up to 2 weeks.

Note
You could even use all three versions of the taratoor for a striking visual impression. The flavours definitely complement each other.

Clockwise from left:
Taratoor (page 42),
Red taratoor (page 43),
Green taratoor (page 43)

Opposite page, left to right:
Lemon dressing (page 46),
Sweet-and-sour dressing
(page 47), Pomegranate
dressing (page 46)

LEMON DRESSING

·All recipes pictured on page 45

This is a very simple lemon dressing that can be used on many different salads, but specifically for the Iceberg and walnut taratoor (page 116) and Winter fattoush (see page 120).

Place all the ingredients in a jar or container with a tight-fitting lid. Seal firmly and shake, shake, shake!
  Store in the fridge for up to 1 month.

Makes 300 ml (10½ fl oz)

100 ml (3½ fl oz) lemon juice
100 ml (3½ fl oz) extra-virgin olive oil
100 ml (3½ fl oz) canola oil
½ teaspoon salt

POMEGRANATE DRESSING

The use of pomegranate molasses in dressings is one of the earliest 'modern Middle Eastern' influences I remember that came from Greg Malouf's kitchen. Pre-mixed dressings are not the norm in the Middle East, and specific ingredients are often narrowly assigned to particular dishes. For example, a pomegranate molasses dressing is really only found on fattoush, despite its rise in popularity as a classic 'Middle Eastern' dressing.

Combine all the ingredients in a jar or container with a tight-fitting lid. Seal, and give it a good shake. Store in the fridge for up to 3 months.

Makes 280 ml (9½ fl oz)

80 ml (⅓ cup) extra-virgin olive oil
80 ml (⅓ cup) canola oil
30 ml (1 fl oz) pomegranate molasses
50 ml (1¾ fl oz) red wine vinegar
½ teaspoon salt

SWEET-AND-SOUR DRESSING

This dressing is a little complex. It was inspired by the Iranian tradition of dipping cos leaves into Sekanjabin (page 28), which is a syrup made from sugar, mint and vinegar. To turn this into a balanced dressing that maintained the essence of that tradition, I lightened it with the addition of verjuice and lemon.

Makes 340 ml (11½ fl oz)

85 ml (2¾ fl oz) verjuice
85 ml (2¾ fl oz) Sekanjabin (page 28)
70 ml (2¼ fl oz) extra-virgin olive oil
70 ml (2¼ fl oz) canola oil
30 ml (1 fl oz) lemon juice
½ teaspoon salt

Place all the ingredients in a jar or container with a tight-fitting lid and shake, shake, shake!
   Store in the fridge for up to 1 month.

SAFFRON WATER

· *Recipe pictured on page 48*

Turning your saffron threads into a water that is potent and ready to use will change your life! Well, maybe not your life, but it will definitely change how and when you use saffron. This method of toasting then grinding into a genuine saffron powder also extends the yield you get from a very expensive ingredient. It lasts weeks if not months in the fridge and is great to have on hand to use in anything from rice to ice cubes.

Makes 200 ml (7 fl oz)

1 g (⅕₂ oz) saffron
½ teaspoon sugar

Lightly toast the saffron in a dry frying pan over a medium heat until fragrant. Do not allow it to darken in colour. You want to just warm the saffron gently to dry it a little further.
   Remove from the pan and place in a mortar and pestle or spice grinder with the sugar. Grind the saffron and sugar to a fine powder and tip into a glass jar.
   Boil 200 ml (7 fl oz) water and tip it into the jar over the saffron. Seal with a lid and, once cooled, store in the fridge for future use. It will keep for up to 2 weeks.

NOTES

On deep-frying

Deep-frying has a bit of a bad reputation as it is most commonly associated with processed fast food, but it is a key part of many cuisines, Middle Eastern being one of those. Whether it is frying sweet or savoury filled pastries, bittersweet dark brown vegetables or crispy onions, a pot of oil or a deep-fryer are never too far away. A neutral oil like cottonseed or canola works best, as it can handle higher temperatures, and I highly recommend an electric benchtop fryer. Even a tiny domestic fryer from a department store will make life easier. In the absence of that, I suggest you heat a pot of oil on the stove to around 180°C (350°F), but bear in mind that a pot on the stove can be a fire hazard, whereas a small deep-fryer will have a safety cut-off. One time in a commercial kitchen I forgot the pot of oil on the stove. It got so hot it popped the mercury cooking thermometer. I nearly peed my pants!

On crisping flatbread

My favourite way to crisp day-old flatbread is to deep-fry it, but for those who would prefer not to, you can toast it any way you like, be that in an oven, a toaster or on the barbecue at the end of your cook-up as my mum does. If you are deep-frying, cut the bread into squares or triangles around 2 cm (¾ in) wide and fry until light brown as they will continue to colour after you remove them from the oil. Season with salt, then set aside. If crisping in the oven, leave the bread whole, toast it for a few minutes until browned, then break it into the salad. You could brush the bread with a little olive oil and season with salt and sumac, too. Once toasted, both of these will last days if not weeks in an airtight container.

RUMI: THE STORY OF a RESTAURANT

My travels through the Middle East gave me an appreciation of long afternoons sipping tea, puffing on a hookah pipe and enjoying Middle Eastern music. This became a source of inspiration as I thought about opening my own venue: a small tea bar that played Middle Eastern music, served up hubbly bubbly hookah pipes and a mix of my own Middle Eastern-inspired dishes and Mum's food that would come from the endless supply of frozen goodies she has in case a small army happens to call by without notice. My first idea was a bar called Hookahs and Tea (a name which seemed to impress only me) – a very early, very simple idea that evolved to become the restaurant that took its name from Rumi, the mystic poet-philosopher. Rumi was born in Afghanistan (at the time part of Greater Persia), wrote in Persian and Arabic, and settled in Turkey. Like Rumi, the poet, the focus of the restaurant would be on the common thread running through the Middle East rather than the differences. The food would be inspired by my Lebanese heritage, with a nod to the influences of Turkish cuisine, as well as an exploration of Persian cuisine that I was starting to understand had influenced the food of the whole region, stretching from Afghanistan all the way to Morocco. Rumi, the restaurant, was born.

Around this time, I met Natalie, the woman who was to become my wife and who, as she has done throughout our whole relationship, supported me to back myself, and volunteered to run the front of house. The journey began to find a site for a restaurant where I would focus on developing ideas around how I thought Middle Eastern food could be cooked and presented. On a very tight budget, I searched for an existing business that was looking to move on rather than build from scratch. This proved difficult because, as I was to learn, people selling businesses, whether profitable or not, attach an inflated value to them. I visited so many sites in the inner north of Melbourne looking for the right fit. I remember one place in particular that brought me to tears when I missed out on the lease. I thought I'd missed my big chance. I quickly realised that this tiny place that would have seated around 20 people and didn't even have a toilet may not have been the golden opportunity that I was looking for. I kept on searching, eventually resorting to slipping notes under the doors of shops that I thought could work, until I received a call from a cocky Italian guy named Massimo about his restaurant (named Massimo) in Lygon Street, East Brunswick.

He wanted a lot of money for a business that made none, but we were eventually able to reach an agreement with the help of my long-time friend, mentor and former employer, Tony Fazio. It was more than I wanted to pay, but time was ticking and the venue had good bones. Instantly charming, too. Rumi, East Brunswick was born.

This was 2006. The internet was a chore, the iPhone had not yet been released and there was a brothel three doors down. There wasn't much going on in East Brunswick, which suited me because I thought if I completely messed things up, nobody would notice. The brothel turned out to be quite useful as the only recognisable landmark for people I was giving directions to; everyone seemed to know The Lodge. The madam even doubled up as barista at a cafe called Small Block, the only sign of gentrification in the area, which happened to be on the adjacent corner. As we began our renovations, everything from resurfacing the floors and walls, restoring tables and chairs and lots and lots of painting was mostly done by my dad, Jack, my girlfriend Nat and myself, with the incredibly generous help of siblings, cousins, friends, future in-laws and aunties who chipped in to do whatever they could. Of course, Mum kept everyone fed.

The front door was painted the day we opened. There was no media release. No socials (they didn't really exist yet). No website (same). No money (hello, credit card). But there was passion, youth, hard work, love, support and prayers, not to mention the fear of losing my life's savings.

Our first trial run was a disaster, which resulted in me delaying the official opening day so I could gather my thoughts and find out why nobody had told me that I couldn't cook. Had my friends and family just gone along with this because they didn't want to hurt my fragile feelings? Surely Nat, who isn't known for mincing her words, would have told me. Fortunately, it turned out that I just needed a bit of time to swap hats from restaurant builder to restaurant chef.

The biggest challenge now was getting what was in my head onto the plate. Even though I'd had an inspirational stint at MoMo, I was trying to create a casual venue similar to the well-known Ladro in Fitzroy under Rita Macali that served the highest-quality Italian food. There was no Rumi to work at before Rumi opened, and the Melbourne dining scene had barely shifted off its fine-dining course. Every dish was a process of trial and error, whether it was cooking on charcoal in a commercial setting (almost unheard of in 2006) or using colourful mismatched plates (collected from op shops) rather than the standard whites that were ubiquitous. There was also the idea of a 'shared table' where set dishes for each customer were replaced by a series of sharing plates in the middle of the table. It was quite a challenge getting people to accept such changes and, at one point, we resorted to likening the experience to dining at a Chinese restaurant, hoping to give some comfort to the guests who were concerned about missing out. The same applied to the pushback over not serving 'normal' coffee. When I tried to explain that the 'normal' coffee they were used to was Italian espresso and that, in fact, coffee is an Arabic word, I was met with blank stares. Again we resorted to the Chinese dining analogy, explaining that just as you don't serve Italian coffee in a Chinese restaurant, you wouldn't expect to find it in a Middle Eastern restaurant. Not everyone was convinced by this and a few left quite disappointed. Two customers in particular stuck out. The first was a guest who was so upset by our offering Middle Eastern coffee that, when leaving in a huff, told us that we 'won't last long around here'. The second was a guest who asked why I wasn't wearing a tea towel on my head when I delivered him his coffee. Luckily, they were a tiny minority.

We must have been doing something right because the people kept coming, slowly but surely. As we attracted the attention of the food media and word started to spread, my parents' concerns over me not serving steak or pasta in case people didn't like 'our' food were gradually alleviated.

One particular article really got things moving. It was a Friday night around 6.30 pm. The restaurant was empty and we had very few bookings. The staff and I were sitting up the back killing time and chatting to our neighbour, Hugh, who, with his mother Lisa, was about to open a bar next door called The Alderman. His dog, who went everywhere with him, was standing at the front door waiting for Hugh. A couple of kids in school uniform with their mum had to move the dog out of the way to enter the restaurant. My heart sank. Not only were there barely any bookings, two of the walk-ins were kids who weren't going to spend much. We dispersed to fulfil our roles: Nat to greet the guests warmly, Hugh to keep working on his bar and me to go back to the kitchen to sweat over paying the bills. As I turned around to look at the dining room, I realised that a man who had just joined the family was head reviewer for *The Age* newspaper, and he was writing a column for a glossy lift-out of the paper called *The Melbourne Magazine* in which there was a full-page restaurant review, titled HOT SPOT, as well as a page for a few notable dishes that he had eaten that month. I thought, *If he enjoys just one of the dishes tonight, surely it will be worthy of a mention.* It turned out that he was impressed by more than one dish. He loved it all! We were going to be that month's HOT SPOT!

After that, the media attention grew beyond my wildest expectations, and as we were featured in article after article the crowds grew, too. When I appeared on the front cover of the *Good Weekend Magazine* as an up-and-coming chef to watch, the excitement reached a new level. For a short while we got so

> "When I tried to explain that 'normal' coffee was Italian espresso and that coffee was an Arabic word, I was met with blank stares."

busy that we would have to come in on our day off to switch answering machines to handle the enquiries. This, of course, was a time before online bookings existed. What began as a restaurant staffed by me, Nat, an apprentice and a couple of casuals was turning into something a whole lot bigger.

We were thrilled when, in 2009, Matt Preston brought the late Anthony Bourdain to Rumi to film his program *No Reservations*. We still have customers asking for 'what Anthony Bourdain had' and when these requests ramp up, we can comfortably assume that the program is being re-run on SBS, or is being watched on Qantas flights bringing international tourists to our doors.

Night after night the crowds kept coming and we kept selling out of food. It took me quite some time to get used to the idea that we were going to be so busy. There would be people lining up every night at 6 pm looking to get a table and we would unfortunately have to turn them away. There was nowhere nearby they could go.

The continued popularity made it very hard to operate from a tiny space. The size of the restaurant was fine, but the back of house was a pressure cooker. We even had to store produce at home because of the lack of space. This was compounded by a landlord who got a little too involved in our operation while living upstairs. After negotiations for more space failed, in 2009 we took the opportunity to move a block down the road to a larger site.

This brought new challenges as we left the small and charming original site – now housing my friend Alfredo (Freddy) La Spina's Bar Idda – for a larger corner that felt a little more luxe. Once again family and friends chipped in to help convert what had been a mirrored, disco-style restaurant into Rumi mark II.

We quickly adapted to the new space and were able to grow our business once again, opening seven nights and catering for the larger groups that our food is suited to.

This may all sound like it was gruelling, but we have always experienced satisfaction as a family through hard work. We often reflect fondly on the renovation of the restaurant when we see photos of Nat painting the walls when seven months pregnant with our second son Patrick, while our first son Malachy was toddling about and precariously balancing on the ladder his pregnant mother was on. Maybe this ethos is what makes us reflect so fondly each year on the anniversary of our opening. In particular, our tenth birthday party was a great way to celebrate with our family, our staff and the many regular customers who have become friends over the years.

As I write this, I am in the planning stages of realising Rumi in its third and, hopefully final, incarnation. Knowing that our large corner site on Lygon Street was soon going to be sold to developers, I faced the reality of yet another move or retiring the restaurant. This knowledge sat quietly at the back of my mind, often moving to the front as For Sale signs came and went. A chance introduction to the developers of East Brunswick Village had them ask if I was interested in taking over the ground floor of their latest building. As you read this you will know that I said yes, because you can now visit us at Rumi in the East Brunswick Village on Nicholson Street, East Brunswick.

For so long, I dreamed about opening a Middle Eastern restaurant and talked about it to anyone who would listen. I persevered and, with the support of so many people, my dream has become a reality that still surprises me to this day.

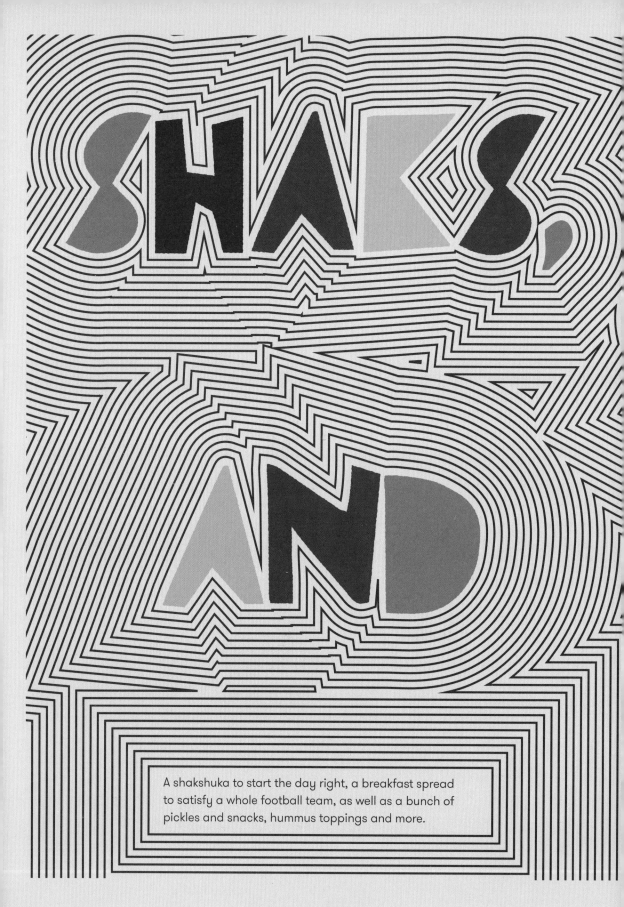

SHAKS, AND

A shakshuka to start the day right, a breakfast spread to satisfy a whole football team, as well as a bunch of pickles and snacks, hummus toppings and more.

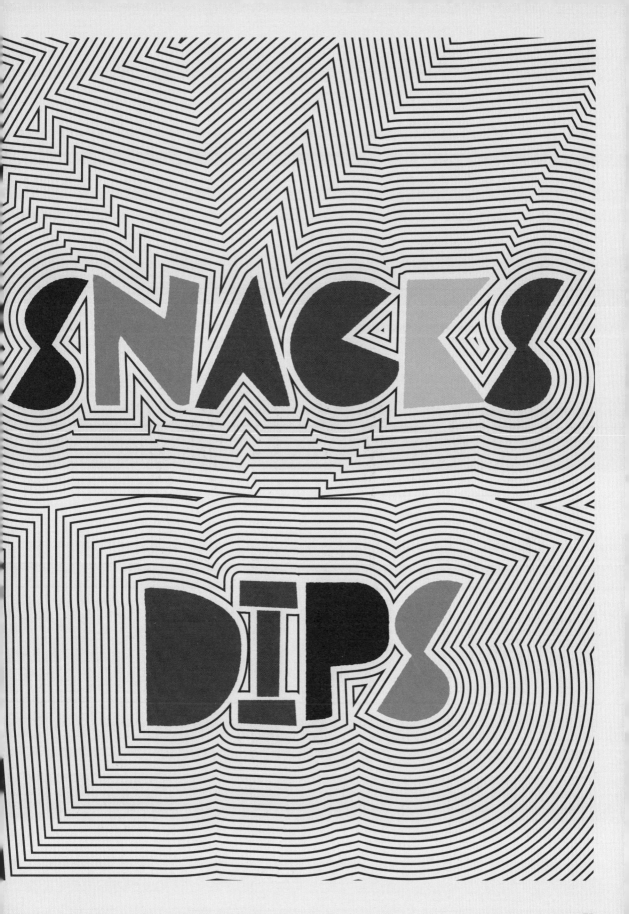

SNACKS

DIPS

SHAKSHUKA

In our first year we offered breakfast on Saturday mornings. The restaurant would be booked twice over in advance for dinner and all but empty for breakfast. We listed this dish on the menu as baked eggs, trying not to freak out a dining public that was just getting used to the idea of breakfast that didn't contain bacon or hollandaise sauce. We still managed to upset one memorable guest, who left almost in tears saying that she 'just wanted some breakfast'. Within a few years, any breakfast joint that took itself seriously was offering shakshuka. We had opted out of the breakfast game by then.

For the sauce, heat the oil in a saucepan over a medium–high heat then add the capsicum and onion with a pinch of salt. Stir for a minute or so then add the garlic and chilli. Stir, then reduce the heat, cover with a lid and cook on low, stirring occasionally. You are looking to soften the onion and capsicum and have them release their sugars. This should take around 20 minutes over a low heat.

Once softened, add the Salça. Stir the paste through the vegetables and cook for a further 5 minutes, stirring occasionally.

Add the tomatoes, stir through and increase the heat to medium–high. When the sauce begins to boil, turn the heat to low and cook with the lid off for around 30 minutes. You can save this sauce for a later date (it will keep in the fridge for a week) or use it right away.

To bake your eggs, preheat your oven to 180°C (350°F).

Heat the sauce in a suitably sized frying pan (that won't melt in your oven). You want to stir the sauce around a little to achieve an even heat, not just boil around the edges.

Once the sauce is near boiling point, turn the heat to low and crack the eggs into the pan, spacing them out. Allow the heat to come back into the sauce and when you start to see the whites of the eggs begin to form, place in the oven for about 5 minutes until the whites are cooked but the yolks are still soft.

In the meantime, melt your Salça butter on the stove or in the microwave. Remove the pan from the oven and top with the feta, parsley and Salça butter. Serve with crusty bread.

Serves 6–8

60 ml (¼ cup) extra-virgin olive oil

1 red capsicum (pepper), deseeded and finely sliced

1 onion, finely sliced

pinch of salt

2 garlic cloves, finely sliced

1 red chilli, deseeded and finely chopped

1 tablespoon Salça (red pepper paste)

200 g (7 oz) tinned chopped tomatoes

8 eggs

2 tablespoons Salça butter (page 28)

50 g (1¾ oz) feta of your choice, crumbled

20 flat-leaf parsley leaves, shredded

crusty bread, to serve

Q. I have some leftover m'nazleh sauce from page 134, could I bake eggs in that?
A. Absolutely! That would be delicious. Really, you can bake eggs in so many different leftovers, but tomato-based sauces – even if they have pasta in them from the previous night's dinner – work particularly well.

SMASHED EGGS

Smashed eggs kept me growing during my teen years while Mum and Dad were at work. It took me years to learn that the secret is to sprinkle the eggs with salt just before serving as well as during the cooking. They're not officially called 'smashed eggs', but we've nicknamed them so because they're pretty much fried eggs that you smash just before serving. Delicious eaten with flatbread.

Serves 3–4

2 tablespoons extra-virgin
  olive oil
6 eggs
salt flakes

Heat the oil in a heavy-based frying pan over a medium–high heat.

Crack your eggs into the pan and sprinkle with a little salt, allowing them to fry in the hot oil creating bubbly, crispy edges.

Just as the whites set, you can smash them up a little with a wooden spoon or using some bread if you're eating with flatbread.

Sprinkle with more salt just before serving.

CRUDITÉS

Raw vegetables are an integral part of the Middle Eastern table and are often served on a platter with a knife to cut your own. This is less of a recipe and more of a reminder that the classic 'chip and dip' is such a refreshing starter to a meal, or a great snack.

Some ideas for crudités:

CUCUMBERS
I prefer the smaller, drier Lebanese (short) cucumbers that can be simply split lengthways or quartered. I don't peel them.

RADISHES
Long ones, round ones, red ones, purple ones. Radishes are a great addition to your crudités as they provide colour, freshness and sometimes a spicy kick. Split the radishes in half top to bottom. If they're small, you can leave them whole. Leave a few leaves attached for extra flair, and these can also be eaten.

CARROTS
Classic. Crunchy, crunchy. Vibrant and sweet. Try washed baby carrots (just a little fatter than a pencil) that can be eaten whole or halved lengthways.

FENNEL
You don't have to buy baby fennel, but you really want to make sure that the fennel is young and in season. Cut into six or seven wedges or separate the fennel ribs.

BABY COS LETTUCE
Baby cos really puts some bulk into a crudité plate. Cut lengthways into wedges.

TOMATOES
Fresh, juicy tomatoes, either halved or left whole, add some fruitiness to the whole offering.

FRESH HERBS
A classic Persian crudité plate is made up of mostly fresh herbs as well as radish and spring onions (scallions), soft white cheese like feta, and walnuts. You can use herbs, such as parsley, mint, basil and dill, leaving them on their crunchy stems. Soak herbs for 10 minutes before serving, then shake dry. There are normally a few damaged leaves towards the bottom of the stems, so pick those off and discard before trimming the stems.

Note
Cutting the vegetables as close as possible to serving them is the key to making such simple food so delicious.

Sprinkle with crunchy salt flakes just before you serve, or offer a dish of salt flakes alongside the crudités.

A little sprinkle of nigella seeds gives the crudités a bit of a kick and also provides a contrasting garnish.

The dip part of this 'chip and dip' could be Labne (page 31), Taratoor (page 42) or Almond taratoor (page 85) served in bowls.

THE BREAKFAST SPREAD

Middle Eastern breakfast, as with most Middle Eastern meals, is more of a spread of dishes that come together to be grazed upon as opposed to having your own complete dish. The following are some of the foods that you may find on the table. There are many other more elaborate dishes that are consumed for breakfast, normally at specialty restaurants. If you're eating out, you'll find anything from kunefé sandwiches (essentially an elaborate grilled cheese sandwich) to za'atar pizzas and fatteh (a dish of toasted bread, chickpeas and yoghurt).

OLIVES
The most common olives in Lebanese cuisine are the small cracked green olives that are pickled in brine (see page 73). You're more likely to find dried black olives in a Turkish breakfast.

LABNE (PAGE 31)
There is always labne, drizzled with plenty of extra-virgin olive oil.

ROLLED LABNE BALLS (PAGE 77)

WHITE CHEESE
Bulgarian sheep's milk feta is probably the most common type of white cheese that you'll find. Danish feta (which I don't rate because it's most commonly a processed cheese) also finds a place.

BREAD
Bread will differ from country to country, but the Lebanese breakfast will always have flatbread that you use to scoop up your food.

JAMS
Fig and sesame, quince, rose, sour cherry.

FRESH VEGETABLES
Most commonly you'll find tomatoes and cucumbers cut into big chunks and sprinkled with salt.

TAHINI AND MOLASSES
This is the most interesting of the breakfast spread and it must be the original PB&J (peanut butter and jelly). It's a mix of tahini and molasses, such as grape, carob or date.

There are a couple of ways to do this. You could simply pour some tahini onto a plate and pool or drizzle with your molasses of choice to scoop up with fresh bread, or you could mix the two in a jar beforehand and use as a spread.

SMASHED EGGS (PAGE 61)

ejjeh

· Recipe pictured on page 68

A thin Lebanese omelette that could almost be called a crêpe. It can be eaten at any time of the day, but it's most enjoyable at breakfast or brunch alongside some Brined green olives (page 73), Labne (page 31) and fresh cucumbers. Of course, Lebanese flatbread, too.

Serves 2–3

3 eggs

1 spring onion (scallion), finely sliced

¼ bunch of flat-leaf parsley, finely chopped

1 teaspoon Baharat (page 24)

1 teaspoon salt

1 tablespoon plain (all-purpose) flour

60 ml (¼ cup) extra-virgin olive oil

Place all the ingredients, except the flour and oil, into a bowl and whisk.

Gradually add the flour while whisking, then allow to rest for 10 minutes.

Heat 1 tablespoon of the oil in a frying pan or crêpe pan over a medium heat. When you can smell the olive oil heating up and just before it starts to smoke, place a 100 ml (3½ fl oz) ladle of the ejjeh mix in the pan, allowing it to spread out like a pancake.

After about 1 minute, flip the ejjeh to colour the other side. Remove from the pan and place on a plate lined with paper towel. Repeat, adding 1 tablespoon oil before cooking each crêpe, until you have used all the mixture.

Top to bottom: Ejjeh (page 67), Labne (page 31), Brined green olives (page 73)
Opposite page: Sigara boregi (page 70)

SIGARA BOREGI

· Recipe pictured on page 69

Cheese-filled bite-sized pastries appear all over the Middle East. This version is inspired by the Turkish one, and translates to cheese 'cigarette', which doesn't sound very appetising when you say it in English. More importantly, the reference is to the long skinny form of these as opposed to the fatter or even triangular shapes found elsewhere. Traditionally they are made with a thick filo called yufka, but we make ours with a store-bought filo available at almost any supermarket or Middle Eastern/Greek grocery store. In this recipe I use three types of cheese, which creates a nice mix of textures and flavours.

Combine the cheeses and oregano in a bowl (this could be done days in advance).

Lay 10 sheets of pastry flat on a chopping board and cut into even strips approximately 10–12 cm (4–4½ in) wide.

Take the last pile of cut pastry and cut that in half lengthways, 5–6 cm (2–2½ in) wide.

You should now have a pile of pastry 10–12 cm (4–4½ in) wide and a pile 5–6 cm (2–2½ in) wide. The narrow strips will be used to help trap the cheese inside the sigara as you are rolling them.

Place all the piles under a damp tea towel so they don't dry out as you make the individual sigara.

To roll the pastries, lay one piece of the wider pastry vertically on your board and lay one piece of narrower pastry horizontally over the top, creating an upside-down cross. It can be difficult to handle single pieces of filo pastry, but keeping the pastry at room temperature will help with this.

Place a heaped tablespoon of the cheese mix in the middle of the horizontal piece, spreading the cheese until it is close to the edge of the wider vertical strip of pastry. Fold the ends of the horizontal piece over to cover the cheese, fold the bottom of the vertical piece up and over the cheese, then roll it all into a cigarette shape, sealing the edge with your finger dipped in water.

Repeat, repeat, repeat …

When you are ready to cook, preheat the oil in your saucepan or deep-fryer to 180°C (350°F) and fry the pastries a few at a time for around 2 minutes. Remove from the oil and drain on paper towel.

Once they are made, you can store the sigara in the fridge, covered with a cloth, for up to 5 days, or in the freezer for 1 month but, ideally, they are best eaten as soon as they are made.

Serves 2–3

100 g (3½ oz) kasseri cheese, grated
100 g (3½ oz) feta, crumbled
100 g (3½ oz) haloumi, grated
1 teaspoon dried oregano
10 sheets filo pastry
oil, for deep-frying (see page 49)

Note

If you are using store-bought filo, it may be frozen. Follow the packet instructions to defrost the pastry and bring it to room temperature before you start cutting and rolling.

You could bake these if you prefer, but they're just not as delicious.

You can omit any of the cheeses, or experiment with what you have on hand, but just ensure you have a total weight of 300 g (10½ oz).

You will have more pastry in a packet than you need for this recipe. You could turn the recipe into a fun exercise for a few people, using up the whole packet then freezing the sigara for a later date. To cook from frozen, simply remove from the freezer and fry when you need them.

SIMPLE PICKLING LIQUID

Pickling was once a technique reserved for preserving food. For example, in the mountains of Lebanon during the height of winter the heavy snow meant that there was no way of growing your own vegetables and often no way to go out to buy fresh goods even if they did somehow manage to make it up the mountain.

Luckily for us, pickling is now mostly done by choice because we've come to appreciate the flavour of pickled foods, especially as an accompaniment to richer dishes. Their acidity can really lift a simple sandwich, salad or barbecued meat. This pickling liquid can pretty much be used on anything. If you enjoy this and feel you want to learn more about pickling, it may be worth checking out a book called Mouneh by Barbara Massaad, or one of the books from the team at Cornersmith in Sydney.

Bring 600 ml (21 fl oz) water, the vinegar and salt to the boil in a saucepan, then turn off the heat and allow to cool.

While the liquor is cooling, prepare your vegetables. Cut the vegetables into small pieces of any shape you like. You can cut small carrots on an angle, leave baby carrots whole, cut turnips into half-moons, or make small florets of cauliflower.

Choose a sterilised jar or container (see page 73) that fits the vegetables without leaving too much space. Add the vegetables and pour in enough pickling liquid to cover the vegetables by about 1 cm (½ in). Seal tightly and refrigerate. Once opened, use within 3 months.

Makes 1.5 litres (6 cups)

225 ml (7¾ fl oz) white wine vinegar
35 g (1¼ oz) salt
600 g (1 lb 5 oz) vegetables (cauliflower, carrot, turnip)

Note
If you are pickling for preservation or you plan to store these on a shelf, you will need to bring a large pot of water to the boil and sterilise your utensils and jars beforehand.

Try adding whole spices, such as peppercorns, whole allspice and aniseed to the jar along with the vegetables. For a bright pink variation, add a roughly diced beetroot (beet) when pickling turnips, cauliflower or other white vegetables. You can also try pickling green almonds for a variation on vegetables.

Add a garlic head split crossways – no need to peel.

If you can, get your hands on some unripe grapes when they are very hard and sour and around the size of a large pea. You may get these off a neighbourhood vine or when visiting a grape farm or winery.

Any leftover pickling liquid makes a great brine for chicken. Submerge the chicken overnight. Remove from the liquid and cook the following day.

BRINED GREEN OLIVES

Olive pickling day (more so, weekend) is my family's version of Looking for Alibrandi's 'national wog day' where we get as many hands on deck to work (except, of course, Mum and Dad always do the most work and the kids grumble). In anticipation of the pickling, my dad goes on a hunt around the creeks looking for wild fennel to flavour the brine.

Makes 1 kg (2 lb 4 oz)

1 kg (2 lb 4 oz) whole unpitted green olives
70 g (2½ oz) salt
sticks of wild fennel (or 1 bunch of dill)
lemon leaves
extra-virgin olive oil

Crack the olives with a mallet or slit individually down one side with a sharp knife, but leave the pits in. Soak in water for 2 days, changing the water halfway.

Prepare the brine by simply mixing the salt with 500 ml (2 cups) water.

Drain the olives and place in sterilised storage jars (jars with narrow collars work best for preserving olives), then pour in the brine. Cut the fennel into 10 cm (4 in) lengths, or leave the dill whole. Tear or cut the lemon leaves into halves or thirds. Add the fennel and lemon leaves and pour in enough olive oil to create a cap of oil about 2 mm (1⁄16 in) above the olives.

The bitterness of the olives will subside, and they will be ready to eat in about 2–3 months. If they are still too bitter for your liking, just leave them a bit longer. Unopened, these olives will last for up to 2 years in a cool, dark cupboard. Once opened, store in the fridge for up to 6 months.

Note
To sterilise your jars, simply bring a large pot of water to the boil and place your jars and utensils in it. Turn off the heat and leave to cool. Jar lids can be washed in hot soapy water then placed on a clean tea towel to dry.

Left to right: Simple pickles (see page 72), Brined green olives (page 73)

ROLLED LABNE BALLS

These rolled labne balls were traditionally made as part of a 'mouneh', which means 'provisions'. Now they can be enjoyed as a fresh morsel to have on hand to add to cheese plates. You can roll them in all sorts of ingredients, which makes for some interesting variations.

Makes 12–16 balls

400 g (14 oz) Labne (page 31)
lots of extra-virgin olive oil

Coating options
Dukkah (page 25)
Za'atar
Sumac
Turkish chilli powder (isot and maras)
Sesame seeds
Nigella seeds

Start by straining the yoghurt for longer than you would for regular labne. It should hang for 3–5 days, and when the labne becomes dry enough to break off a piece, it is ready to roll.

Take a piece approximately 25 g (1 oz), roll into a ball, then gently roll in your chosen coating. Set aside. Repeat until you have rolled all the labne.

The balls can be left plain but, ultimately, the most beautiful preparation for these is rolling them in different coatings and dropping them into a jar of olive oil.

To store them in oil, half-fill a small jar or container with your favourite extra-virgin olive oil, then gently place the balls in the jar. Ensure the oil fully covers the labne and they will keep for at least 1 month in the fridge.

Note
You can use all the labne or as much as you want and keep any leftover labne as a dip or spread, or use it in various other recipes from this book. (If it is not already apparent, I love labne.)

You can experiment with flavouring the olive oil. Try gently warming some olive oil to around 50°C (122°F) and adding some aromatics such as freshly peeled split garlic cloves and some fresh thyme. Allow the oil to cool to room temperature before adding the labne balls; the aromatics will continue to flavour the oil. Be sure to avoid letting the oil get too hot; fried garlic is very bitter.

BEER SNACKS

Drinking alcohol in Lebanon is often connected to food, so much so that there are 'set' snacks that accompany specific drinks. I loved sitting down to an ice-cold beer and being served a few nibbles to enjoy with it. Here are a few you could expect.

CARROTS IN LEMON

These can be baby carrots, but you would normally just receive carrot sticks that have been soaked in lemon juice served with a sprinkle of salt.

SOAKED (ACTIVATED) ALMONDS

Long before this was a superfood trend, soaked almonds were being served in the Middle East. In my experience, they were served alongside the carrots in lemon and a beer. Place the almonds in a bowl with a pinch of salt and double the quantity of water. Leave for at least 12 hours before draining and serving.

TERMOS (LUPIN)

I recommend buying jarred lupin, as they take days of soaking/cooking/soaking otherwise. Even if you buy lupin in a jar, it is recommended that you drain and soak in fresh water for at least 1 day.

   When ready to serve, drain and dress with a big squeeze of lemon, a pinch of salt flakes and a sprinkle of ground cumin. To eat them, you pinch open the skin with your teeth and squeeze out the centre, discarding the skin.

HUMMUS AND TOPPINGS

Another hummus recipe, can you believe it? Chickpeas, tahini, lemon, garlic and salt. How hard could it be? Good question. It isn't that hard at all, but as with so many simple foods, the care taken in the process is what makes the difference. And like all simple recipes, it's the little adjustments you make along the way that makes it yours.

All over the Levant hummus is eaten with toppings such as minced lamb and pine nuts or boiled chickpeas. This turns hummus into quite the brunch meal, which is the time it's most often eaten.

The first time I had hummus like this was during my life-changing journey along the Silk Road. I was in Damascus and, as you so often do when travelling, had woken at the crack of dawn and decided to venture out and experience the city as it comes alive. You know the story: you take this turn instead of that turn, you follow a dog down a lane then discover a little old shopkeeper sitting by a steaming pot of something while waiting for the first morning customers. On this occasion, the steaming pot of something was a pot of chickpeas and the little old shopkeeper was selling hummus fresh and warm, topped with more boiled chickpeas, lemon and garlic. My type of breakfast.

Drain the chickpeas and rinse with cold water.

Cook the chickpeas in a pressure cooker with 625 ml (2½ cups) water until very soft, or slowly simmer in a saucepan with a tight-fitting lid until very soft. Drain the chickpeas and reserve the liquid.

While the chickpeas are still hot, blend them in a food processor for 2 minutes with 125 ml (½ cup) of the cooking liquid, then add the salt, ice and oil. Blend again until very smooth.

Add the tahini and blend again for 2 minutes. Add the toum and lemon juice, blending until smooth.

If you made your hummus in advance, remove it from the fridge about half an hour before you need it, return it to the blender and blend for a few minutes. Check the seasoning and serve.

Serves 6–8

250 g (1¼ cups) dried chickpeas, soaked for at least 12 hours with ½ teaspoon bicarbonate of soda (baking soda)

10 g (¼ oz) salt

75 g (2¾ oz) ice

50 ml (1¾ fl oz) extra-virgin olive oil

175 g (6 oz) tahini

10 g (¼ oz) Toum (page 34)

50 ml (1¾ fl oz) lemon juice

Note

Feel free to use some or all of these tips to make your hummus better:

Soak the chickpeas in bicarbonate of soda (baking soda) over 2 days, changing the water several times.

Try to remove some of the excess skins that float to the top when cooked.

Blend the chickpeas while still warm. Blend without adding too much liquid at the beginning. Blend the chickpeas until your machine is about to die. If your machine dies too easily, buy a better machine.

Once made, cover the surface with some plastic wrap or baking paper to avoid a skin forming.

I like to 'whip' the hummus just before serving. This allows it to warm slightly and me to make final adjustments to the seasoning.

Top to bottom: Minced prawn and coriander (page 83), Hummus (see opposite), Minced lamb and pine nut (page 82)

TOPPINGS

·Recipes pictured on page 81

The creaminess of the hummus with toppings of different textures is a real treat. Feel free to experiment with your own combinations of ingredients.

Minced lamb and pine nut

One of the most traditional hummus toppings. Ask for fatty mince.

Heat the oil in a frying pan over a medium–high heat then add the onion and fry until it begins to brown.

If you haven't pre-fried some pine nuts, you could use my mother's trick by adding the raw pine nuts to the onion now. They will fry with the onions. If you have pre-fried the nuts, leave them until last to garnish.

When the pine nuts have also browned, add the mince. This will stop the nuts from burning. Smash up the mince as it cooks and season with the salt and baharat. Cook gently for 5–10 minutes until the liquid evaporates and the mince is frying in fat.

Spread your hummus on a plate or in a wide bowl, making a large indent. Spoon your minced lamb over the top and garnish with sumac and pine nuts.

You can substitute the lamb with beef or chicken.

Serves 6–8

2 tablespoons extra-virgin olive oil or ghee

1 small onion, finely diced

1 teaspoon fried pine nuts (see page 41)

250 g (9 oz) minced (ground) lamb

1 teaspoon salt

½ teaspoon Baharat (page 24)

1 teaspoon ground sumac, to garnish

Minced prawn and coriander

A play on the traditional minced lamb, and based on the 'Bosphorus' pide at the Moor's Head in Melbourne, this version uses prawns (shrimp), garlic and coriander (cilantro).

Serves 6–8

80 ml (⅓ cup) extra-virgin olive oil

1 small onion, finely diced

4 garlic cloves, finely minced

250 g (9 oz) minced (ground) or finely chopped prawns (shrimp)

1 teaspoon salt

½ teaspoon Baharat (page 24)

1 teaspoon Salça (red pepper paste; see Note)

juice of ½ lemon, plus extra to serve (optional)

1 teaspoon Turkish chilli powder, to garnish

¼ bunch of coriander (cilantro), shredded

Note
You could substitute the Salça with tomato paste and a teaspoon of sweet paprika.

Heat the oil in a frying pan over a medium heat then add the onion and fry gently. Add the garlic just before the onion starts to brown and fry for about 10 seconds.

Add the prawns, season with the salt and baharat, then turn the heat down to low and cook for 3–4 minutes, stirring and scraping the bottom of the pan.

Add the Salça and cook for 4–5 minutes, scraping the bottom of the pan. Remove from the heat and deglaze with the lemon juice.

Spread your hummus on a plate or in a wide bowl, making a large indent.

Spoon your minced prawn over the top and garnish with Turkish chilli and fresh coriander leaves, plus an extra squeeze of lemon if you like.

Other options

CHICKPEAS
This is the simplest of toppings, where you simply spoon some warm cooked chickpeas over the hummus and top with plenty of extra-virgin olive oil. An alternative could be to warm the chickpeas in some Salça butter (page 28).

DUKKAH (PAGE 25)
FRIED CAULIFLOWER (PAGE 94)
LEFTOVER SHREDDED LAMB SHOULDER (PAGE 128)
LEFTOVER SHREDDED TAHINI CHICKEN (PAGE 133)
SALÇA BUTTER (PAGE 28)

ALMOND TARATOOR

Almond taratoor has been a hero starter at Rumi for many years now. It's almost a cheat's hummus as the base is almond meal that you can have on hand at any time as opposed to chickpeas, which have to be soaked, cooked and blended. We don't have hummus on the menu at Rumi because it is such a well-known dish and I wanted people to venture a little further than the stock-standard offerings of most Middle Eastern restaurants. If you weren't paying attention, you would swear it was hummus, as many a customer has, but it has a sweeter, denser and obviously nuttier character.

Serves 4–6

2 teaspoons salt

1 tablespoon Toum (page 34)

2 tablespoons tahini

2 tablespoons lemon juice

2 tablespoons extra-virgin olive oil, plus extra to serve

300 g (10½ oz) blanched almond meal

Place all the ingredients, except for the almond meal, in a food processor and pulse for a few seconds to combine, then add half the almond meal and blend until combined. Add 200 ml (7 fl oz) water and blend until combined. Add the remaining almond meal and blend until you think your food processor is going to die. This will take around 5 minutes or more – with occasional pauses to scrape down the side – to produce a beautifully smooth finish. Check the consistency and add a little more water if needed to loosen – the taratoor should be the consistency of hummus. Drizzle with a little olive oil to finish.

This will keep in an airtight container in the fridge for up to 1 week.

Note

To prevent a skin forming, press some greaseproof paper onto the surface of the taratoor until it cools down as it will likely be warm when it comes out of the food processor.

Serve with olive oil and a sprinkle of Dukkah (page 25), if you like.

COLD YOGHURT SOUPS

Not a soup in the traditional sense, but I don't know what else you'd call it. There are two garnish options here. One is the simple Lebanese garnish of cucumber and mint, and the other is the more elaborate and finessed Iranian version. Both are served on hot days as an afternoon snack that refreshes you, post siesta. Of course, this can also be served as an appetiser as part of a larger meal. Use full-fat (whole) natural yoghurt for a boost to your gut health, too!

Lebanese

Place the yoghurt, garlic, salt and ice in a bowl and whisk to create a smooth consistency and dissolve the salt. Stir in the diced cucumber and fresh mint.

Serve in chilled bowls sprinkled with extra diced cucumber and a pinch of dried mint.

Serves 4

300 g (10½ oz) natural yoghurt

1 garlic clove, crushed to a smooth paste, or 1 teaspoon Toum (page 34)

1 teaspoon salt

a few ice cubes

1 cucumber, cut into 5 mm (¼ in) dice, plus extra to garnish

10 fresh mint leaves, finely shredded just before adding to the yoghurt

pinch of dried mint

Iranian

Place the yoghurt, salt and ice in a bowl and whisk to make the yoghurt smooth and dissolve the salt. Stir in the diced cucumber and fresh mint.

Serve in chilled bowls sprinkled with the dried mint, rose, walnuts and sultanas.

Q. Where can I buy dried rose?
A. *Persian or Afghan grocers sell dried rose in petals, which you can grind yourself in a spice grinder or mortar and pestle to make a powder. You can still make this soup without the dried rose if you can't find any.*

Other fragrant herbs such as basil and tarragon also work nicely stirred through with the mint.

Serves 4

300 g (10½ oz) natural yoghurt

1 teaspoon salt

a few ice cubes

1 cucumber, cut into 5 mm (¼ in) dice

10 fresh mint leaves, finely shredded just before adding to the yoghurt

pinch of dried mint

pinch of dried rose powder

80 g (⅔ cup) walnuts, quartered

40 g (1½ oz) sultanas or raisins

OYSTERS WITH PICKLED GRAPE DRESSING

Unripe grapes (known as hossrom) in the Middle East are a traditional source of tartness in the cuisine. Their juice (verjuice) is sour and makes a great substitute for lemon. A less common but still popular preparation in Iran is to pickle them. This recipe is inspired by the classic French oysters mignonette.

Serves 6–12

12 oysters

2 red Asian shallots, peeled and finely chopped

100 g (3½ oz) pickled grapes, finely chopped

1 tablespoon pickle juice (from the pickled grapes)

pinch of freshly cracked black pepper

If the oysters are closed, you will need to shuck them. Or, if you'd prefer, you can ask your fishmonger to do it for you.

Mix all the remaining ingredients in a bowl and serve on the side of the oysters, or top each oyster with a little of the dressing.

You could try pickling your own grapes by using the recipe on page 72 and raiding a neighbour's grape vine when the grapes are still tiny and hard. Alternatively, a Persian grocer will have them.

The Secret Lives of Yoghurt and Tahini

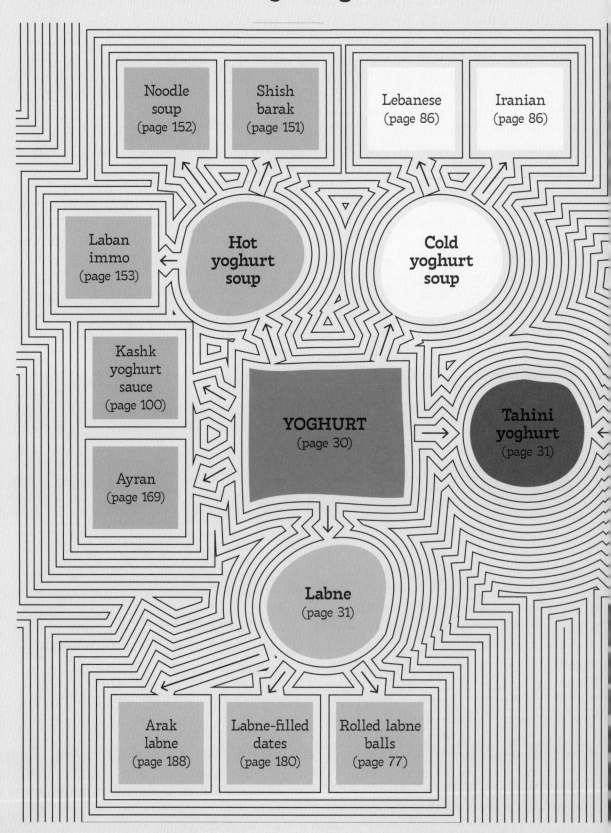

Noodle soup (page 152)

Shish barak (page 151)

Lebanese (page 86)

Iranian (page 86)

Laban immo (page 153)

Hot yoghurt soup

Cold yoghurt soup

Kashk yoghurt sauce (page 100)

YOGHURT (page 30)

Tahini yoghurt (page 31)

Ayran (page 169)

Labne (page 31)

Arak labne (page 188)

Labne-filled dates (page 180)

Rolled labne balls (page 77)

Middle Eastern food makes unique and expert use of these two ingredients. Here are some of the ways they are incorporated into the cuisine, and the recipes in this book.

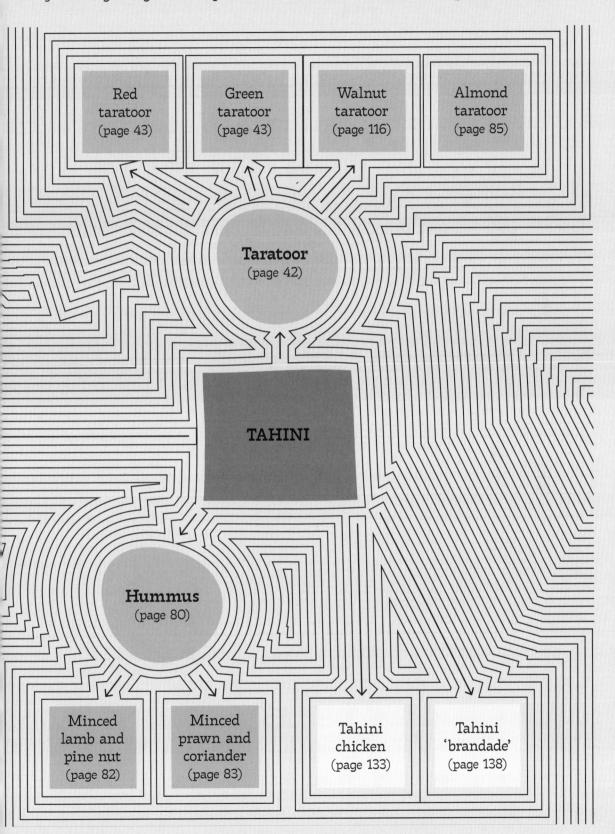

Red taratoor (page 43)

Green taratoor (page 43)

Walnut taratoor (page 116)

Almond taratoor (page 85)

Taratoor (page 42)

TAHINI

Hummus (page 80)

Minced lamb and pine nut (page 82)

Minced prawn and coriander (page 83)

Tahini chicken (page 133)

Tahini 'brandade' (page 138)

CALL SALAD

Too many sad salads are out there ruining the reputations of great vegetables, so please, don't call me that. Middle Eastern food has so many preparations based on veg and grains that are easy to call a salad, but are so much more. Many of them are a meal in their own right, full of wholesome, seasonal and tasty ingredients.

FRIED CAULIFLOWER WITH CARAMELISED ONION, CURRANTS AND PINE NUTS

If you make this dish correctly, you'll be asking yourself if you've burnt it. It's okay. My training in modern European kitchens where everything had to be golden brown had me second-guessing, too. It just doesn't taste the same if it is golden brown. It's that dark bittersweet flavour that transforms cauliflower.

This dish has been on the menu at Rumi since the day we opened and was inspired by Rita Macali's cauliflower at Ladro, then later at Supermaxi. Before that, the only cauliflower you'd find in Melbourne was the unwanted friend of broccoli and carrots at the pub, or at a French restaurant covered in sauce mornay. Melbourne, you've come a long way.

Heat a small frying pan over a low heat and add 2 tablespoons of the vegetable oil and the pine nuts. Fry gently until the pine nuts start to change colour and become golden. At this point, strain through a small sieve and spread them on a plate or tray lined with paper towel. They will continue to colour so be sure to take them off the heat before they get too brown.

Heat the remaining oil in a small saucepan over a high heat until very hot, then add the onion, stirring frequently until it starts to colour. Turn down the heat to low and allow the onion to caramelise slowly. Cook for approximately 30 minutes until completely soft and dark brown. Season with salt and allspice, then add the currants, stirring through the onion until well combined. Remove from the heat.

For the cauliflower, fill a saucepan with heavily salted water and bring to a rolling boil. Cut the cauliflower into florets at least the size of a golf ball and no bigger than a mandarin. Boil in the salted water for 8–10 minutes until soft, then remove from the water with a kitchen spider or strain through a sieve. Spread on a tray lined with paper towel or a tea towel and allow to cool and dry out a little.

When ready to fry, heat the oil in a saucepan or deep-fryer to 180°C (350°F). Dredge the cauliflower in the flour then shake off any excess in a sieve. Fry until dark brown. Yes – DARK!

Remove from the oil and drain on some paper towel. Season with salt and pepper, then arrange on a plate and top with the caramelised onion, currants and pine nuts.

Serves 6–8

100 ml (3½ fl oz) vegetable oil
2 teaspoons pine nuts
2 onions, cut into 2 cm
 (¾ in) squares
salt, to taste
small pinch of ground allspice
1 tablespoon currants
1 small head of cauliflower
oil, for deep-frying (see
 page 49)
plain (all-purpose) flour, for
 dusting

Note
You can use chickpea flour (besan) for dusting for a gluten-free result.

If you prefer to steam (not boil) the cauliflower, that is fine. Be sure to sprinkle with lots of salt before it goes into the steamer.

The onions and the boiling of the cauliflower can be done a few days in advance. Be sure to warm the onion mix slightly before using it.

The pine nuts can also be prepared days in advance. If you have become a fan of frying nuts, you can fry a larger batch. They will keep in the fridge for up to 3 months.

The traditional accompaniment for this fried cauliflower is Taratoor (page 42). Leftover fried cauliflower goes beautifully in a flatbread sandwich drizzled with taratoor.

BaTaTa HaRRa *Spicy potatoes*

This classic Lebanese dish that is often served as part of a mezze spread has become a favourite at Rumi. The recipe is intended to be a guide and an inspiration for flavour combinations rather than a definitive script, so add as much or little flavouring as you like. Saying that, classics become such for a reason and there's something about the coriander (cilantro), chilli and garlic mix that hits the spot.

Serves 6–8

1 kg (2 lb 4 oz) floury potatoes

2 tablespoons salt, plus extra to serve

oil, for deep-frying (see page 49)

2 tablespoons Toum (page 34)

1 teaspoon Aleppo pepper

15 g (½ cup) roughly chopped coriander (cilantro) leaves

Wash the potatoes then cut into 4 cm (1½ in) cubes.

Place the potatoes in a large pot of water with the salt and bring to the boil over a high heat. Reduce the heat to medium-low and simmer. After 3–4 minutes, check that the potatoes are well cooked by sticking a knife into them. There should be very little resistance. Drain the potatoes then spread on a tray to dry out and cool down.

Heat enough oil for deep-frying in a saucepan or deep-fryer to 180°C (350°F) and fry the potatoes until golden brown, about 3–4 minutes. Drain and tip into a mixing bowl with the toum, Aleppo pepper, coriander and an (un)healthy sprinkle of salt. Toss in the bowl a few times then arrange on a plate or platter of your choice.

Note

The potatoes can be boiled ahead of time and refrigerated for up to 2 days if this helps you plan.

Toum can also be prepared ahead of time. In fact, you should always have some on hand!

Overboiled potatoes are ugly and messy but taste the best, so don't stress if you overcook them.

THREE BURNT EGGPLANTS

Burning eggplants (aubergines) may seem strange when you first encounter it, but once you've tasted eggplant prepared this way, you will appreciate that this depth of flavour is only achieved by this seemingly extreme way of cooking. The wonderful bitter-sweetness is created by burning the skin, which provides a protective layer to the flesh inside, which then in turn loses some of its moisture, further concentrating the flavour and texture. This is a dish that can mostly be prepared ahead of time. If you happen to have a barbecue (especially a charcoal barbecue), you can throw the eggplants on at the end of a meal and let them do their thing.

Burnt eggplant

· Recipe pictured on page 102

Start by peeling off the leaves around the neck of the eggplants, then prick them a few times with a pointy knife. I'm not entirely sure why this is done – I assume it's to allow steam to escape – but it is what my mum does, so that's good enough for me.

Place the eggplants directly onto hot charcoal, a barbecue grill, or over a low gas flame and turn occasionally until completely blackened all over.

Once the skin has blackened and the flesh is soft, remove from the heat and sit the eggplants in a colander to drain. When they have cooled enough to handle, carefully peel the skin away with a paring knife, being sure to remove as much skin as possible while keeping the eggplants whole. This is not crucial, but it presents beautifully and the first recipe is called whole baba, not half baba or mushed baba. Seriously, though, you don't have to keep them whole.

Open up the eggplants by sliding your thumb through the flesh, creating a slit to sprinkle salt into. Close them back up and sprinkle a generous amount of salt over the outside as well. Place back in the colander until you are ready to use.

You can use this burnt eggplant as a base to create any of the three meals that follow.

Makes 2

2 whole eggplants (aubergines)
salt, to taste

Note
Don't wash the eggplants after you've burnt them. The flavour that is produced between the skin and flesh far outweighs any little black specs that you may miss when removing the skin.

If you have time, you can put them in a colander for an hour or overnight. This will allow any excess liquid to drain away, further intensifying the flavour and the texture of the eggplant.

Eggplant, the whole baba

·Recipe pictured on page 103

Baba ganoush is a classic Lebanese combination of tahini, lemon, garlic and salt mixed into mashed grilled eggplant (aubergine). This version leaves the eggplant whole. This would have once been written on a menu as a 'deconstructed baba ganoush'. Fortunately, that trend has passed, but I guess it is deconstructed baba ganoush, isn't it?

Serves 4–6

1 × quantity Burnt eggplant (see opposite)
100 ml (3½ fl oz) Taratoor (page 42)
dried mint, to garnish

Garnishes (optional)
1 teaspoon ground sumac
1 teaspoon Aleppo pepper
¼ bunch of shredded flat-leaf parsley
50 g (1¾ oz) Crispy onions (page 36)
50 ml (1¾ fl oz) extra-virgin olive oil

Bring the eggplants to room temperature or warm gently in the oven or in a microwave.

Place the eggplants in a shallow bowl and use a spoon to make a thin slit lengthways down the eggplants. Pour the taratoor into the slits and all over the eggplants.

Top with one or all of the garnishes, if using. Serve in your favourite soup bowls and garnish with dried mint.

Eggplant kashk

· Recipes pictured on page 103

This recipe is inspired by 'kashk e bademjan', a traditional Iranian dish that is a robust dip, but this version also leaves the eggplant (aubergine) whole. Kashk is a fermented and dried full-fat sour milk. You can buy it dry and reconstitute it, or buy it ready made in jars. As with baba ganoush, it is normally served mashed, but I really like this version that we came up with. If you can't find kashk, you can substitute it with Tahini yoghurt (page 31). This recipe will take 3–4 days to make, but it's worth the wait to allow the flavour to really penetrate the eggplant.

For the yoghurt sauce, simply place all the ingredients in a bowl and whisk together until smooth.

Make the marinade by combining all the ingredients in a saucepan and warm gently over a low heat until the garlic just begins to sizzle. Switch off the heat and set the marinade aside for as long as possible – ideally a day or two (you don't need to refrigerate it). Strain the oil using a fine sieve, discarding the other ingredients, and reserve.

Place the burnt eggplants in a container with the flavoured oil, seal and allow to marinate for a day or two in the fridge.

When you're ready to assemble, bring the eggplants in the oil to room temperature or warm gently in the oven or microwave.

Remove the eggplants from the marinade, retaining the oil to use later. Place them in a shallow bowl and use a spoon to open up a thin slit lengthways down the eggplants and scatter the salt into the slits.

Pour the kashk yoghurt sauce into the slits and all over the eggplants. Garnish with the nigella seeds, crispy onions and dried mint, and drizzle 100 ml (3½ fl oz) of the marinade over the top.

Serves 4–6

1 × quantity Kashk yoghurt sauce (see below)

1 × quantity Onion marinade (see below)

1 × quantity Burnt eggplant (page 98)

1 teaspoon salt

pinch of nigella seeds

50 g (1¾ oz) Crispy onions (page 36)

pinch of dried mint, to garnish

Kashk yoghurt sauce
50 g (1¾ oz) kashk

100 g (3½ oz) natural yoghurt

1 tablespoon Toum (page 34), or 1 crushed garlic clove

1 teaspoon salt

Onion marinade
1 large onion, thinly sliced

150 ml (5 fl oz) extra-virgin olive oil

1 teaspoon ground turmeric

1 teaspoon dried mint

2 garlic cloves, thinly sliced

Note
The leftover marinade can be used to drizzle over dips, for frying onions, or it can be used to make a dressing for another dish.

Eggplant with garlic yoghurt, tomatoes and mint

This is not a dish inspired by anywhere in particular but it's bloody delicious. I once presented it at Tawlet restaurant in Beirut as a guest chef. Cooking in Beirut at one of the most highly regarded restaurants in the country of my heritage was most definitely one of the highlights of my career.

Serves 4–6

1 × quantity Yoghurt dressing (see below)

1 × quantity Burnt eggplant (see page 98)

1 tomato, halved lengthways then cut into wedges

¼ red onion, halved lengthways, then cut into very thin crescent-moon shapes

5 mint leaves

20 flat-leaf parsley leaves

½ teaspoon ground sumac

50 ml (1¾ fl oz) extra-virgin olive oil

Yoghurt dressing

200 ml (7 fl oz) natural yoghurt

1 tablespoon Toum (page 34), or 1 crushed garlic clove

½ teaspoon salt

For the dressing, place the yoghurt, toum and salt in a bowl and whisk together.

To assemble, bring the eggplants to room temperature or warm gently in the oven or microwave.

Place the eggplants in a shallow bowl and use a spoon to open up a thin slit lengthways down the eggplants.

Pour the yoghurt dressing into the slits and all over the eggplants. Garnish with the tomato wedges, onion, mint, parsley, sumac and olive oil.

Note
Serve these dishes at room temperature or slightly warm (around 45°C/113°F if you want to be technical).

If you take to toum – as I'm sure you will once you realise how easy it is to make – you'll want to have a tub permanently on hand so you can substitute crushed garlic in any recipe with toum. Just make sure you always replace one quantity of garlic with two quantities of toum.

Clockwise from top: Eggplant with garlic yoghurt, tomatoes and mint (page 101), Eggplant kashk (page 100) Opposite page: Eggplant, the whole baba (page 99)

KOSHARI

· Recipes pictured on page 106

The ultimate carb-loading dish, koshari is Egyptian footballer Mohamed Salah's secret weapon. It's a mix of chickpeas, rice, pasta, lentils and crispy onions, and it's the most popular street food in Egypt, catering to rich and poor alike.

As with many traditional dishes, there are so many ways to prepare koshari. I prefer to cook all the ingredients separately then combine them at the end. I think this gives the best control over the end product. All parts of this recipe can be prepared up to a couple of days before, then put together when needed by reheating. It's a bit of a time-consuming dish, but well worth the effort.

CHICKPEAS

To cook the dried chickpeas, you'll first need to soak them in water overnight with the bicarbonate of soda. The following day, drain and rinse them and place in a large saucepan. Fill the pan with cold water three times the depth of the chickpeas. Bring to the boil, then simmer gently for 30–40 minutes, or until tender. Turn off the heat, add 1 teaspoon salt and leave the chickpeas in the water to cool.

MEDIUM-GRAIN RICE

Wash the rice in two or three changes of water, then drain and set aside. Place in a saucepan with 1.5 litres (6 cups) water and 1 tablespoon of the salt.

Simmer over a medium–high heat to get it going, then lower to medium–low and cook for 3–4 minutes, giving it an occasional gentle stir until it looks like wet porridge.

Turn down to very low and cook with the lid on for 15 minutes.

MACARONI

Cook the pasta according to the packet instructions in plenty of salted boiling water. Drain and set aside.

LENTILS

To cook the lentils, place them in a large saucepan and fill with cold water three times the depth of the lentils. Add 1 teaspoon of the salt, bring to the boil, then simmer gently for about 20 minutes until tender. Remove from the heat and leave the lentils in the water to cool.

THE SAUCE

Heat the olive oil and garlic in a saucepan set over a medium heat until the garlic sizzles, then turn to low ensuring the garlic doesn't burn. Cook for about 1 minute, then stir in the cumin and coriander and sauté for a further 10 seconds before adding the tomatoes. Bring to the boil over a medium–high heat, then simmer the sauce for 20 minutes over medium–low, remembering to stir occasionally. Remove from the heat and add the vinegar.

Serves 8

1 × quantity Crispy onions (page 36)

The carbs

220 g (1 cup) dried chickpeas

pinch of bicarbonate of soda (baking soda)

440 g (2 cups) medium-grain rice

1½ tablespoons salt

155 g (1 cup) short pasta, such as small macaroni

200 g (1 cup) green, brown or puy lentils

The sauce

1 tablespoon extra-virgin olive oil

4 garlic cloves, chopped

1 teaspoon ground cumin

1 teaspoon ground coriander

200 g (7 oz) tinned chopped tomatoes

1 tablespoon white wine vinegar

TO ASSEMBLE

If the chickpeas and lentils have gone cold, reheat them in their liquid before draining. Mix the chickpeas, lentils, pasta and rice in a bowl before spooning onto a serving plate.

Top with the sauce (you could serve this on the side) and the crispy onions.

For a variation, you could add the drained chickpeas and lentils as well as the pasta to the top of the rice just as the rice is almost finished cooking. The steam in the rice pot will heat up the ingredients. When ready to serve, tip out into a bowl and finish with the sauce and crispy onions.

You could also mix all the ingredients together, then microwave before finishing with the toppings.

Note

I like my chickpeas soft so I leave them to cook a little bit longer than a recipe might normally suggest because they harden a little as they cool.

When the chickpeas are simmering, they may produce a foam that will float to the top. This can be skimmed and discarded. Similarly, the skins may float to the top, and they can be discarded or not.

Opposite page: Koshari (pages 104–5)

MUM'S NOODLE RICE

Noodles mixed with rice shouldn't make sense, but it just does. This was the standard rice dish that would accompany any number of stews Mum would make when we were growing up. She often got the base ready so she just needed to add water when we were ready to eat. This recipe was actually created so that my sons could learn how to make their Tayta's (grandmother's) rice, and I had to steal it back from Malachy's iPad.

Serves 4

220 g (1 cup) medium-grain rice

3 tablespoons ghee, or 180 ml (¾ cup) extra-virgin olive oil

50 g (½ cup) vermicelli noodles

1 teaspoon salt

Wash the rice in two or three changes of water. Drain and set aside.

Heat the ghee in a saucepan over a medium–high heat until you can smell it. Reduce the heat to medium then add the noodles. Stir constantly until the noodles are light brown. Add the washed rice to the pan with 500 ml (2 cups) water and the salt.

Simmer over a medium–high heat to get it going, then lower the heat to medium–low and stir occasionally until it looks like wet porridge, about 2 minutes. Reduce the heat to very low, cover with a lid and cook for 15 minutes.

Q. I don't have any ghee, can I use butter?
A. I wouldn't use butter to cook the noodles because the milk solids will burn, but you can use extra-virgin olive oil and spoon some butter over the rice at the end. You could even just cook it with olive oil for a vegan option.

PERSIAN RICE

Rice plays a starring role in Iranian cuisine, from very simple dishes to celebratory ones. Here, I am going to attempt to inspire you to cook rice in a way that is uniquely Persian, with some suggested combinations that you could add to this base. The most notable part of this recipe is the tahdig – the crunchy layer of rice that forms on the bottom of the pot – which is not only the prized part of the meal, but also protects the rice from burning.

Soak the rice for half an hour, then drain and rinse a couple of times.

Bring a large saucepan of water to the boil with the salt. Add the drained rice and leave over a high heat until the rice starts to float. Turn it down to low and cook, uncovered, for about 6–8 minutes.

When the rice is just cooked (it should have a tiny crunch in the centre of the grain when chewed) turn off the heat, add 250 ml (9 fl oz) cold water then gently strain through a fine colander. Leave to cool while you prepare the tahdig.

Heat a pot (that will fit your piece of flatbread at the bottom) over a medium–high heat and add the ghee, then top with your piece of bread, laying it flat across the bottom.

Gently add the boiled rice to the pot on top of the bread.

You can add some pieces of butter here to melt into the rice if you like. Place the lid on the pot. The traditional method is to line the lid with a tea towel to catch any condensation. I don't find this crucial but feel free. What you do need is a tight-fitting lid to create steam around the rice. After a few minutes, turn down the heat to very low and steam for 20 minutes. (Don't be tempted to open the lid to check the rice as this will allow all the steam to escape.) Turn off and let it stand for 5 minutes before turning out, upside down, onto a platter. One way to do this is to place the platter on the saucepan and flip it over (carefully) so the tahdig is looking up at you all golden, buttery and crunchy. The tahdig can be cut up into pieces to be shared. Top with the flaked almonds and crispy onions.

Serves 6

400 g (2 cups) basmati rice, or Iranian varieties that you may find at an Afghan or Persian grocer

80 g (2¾ oz) salt

3 tablespoons ghee

1 flatbread

flaked almonds and Crispy onions (page 36), to garnish

Note
Once you are comfortable with this method, try these additions to the rice base. These can be added at the end of the cooking process or layered through as you place the boiled rice into the pot to steam:
   julienned carrots and green raisins
   walnuts and brown raisins
   dried apricots and almonds
   broad beans and finely chopped dill

Or you could go all out and make jewelled rice by adding all of these:
   barberries
   pistachio kernels
   green raisins
   Saffron water (page 47)
   Advieh (page 24)
   julienned carrots (lightly sautéed)

FREEKEH, FETA & POMEGRANATE SALAD

Freekeh is wheat, picked green (young) and then toasted or smoked. It comes from the Arabic word farik, which refers to the rubbing of the grains to remove their husks. It's highly nutritious and it seems the more you eat, the better you feel.

Traditionally, freekeh is used to make hot dishes as if it were rice, but one of the many blessings of being brought up in Australia is that we are not bound by such traditions and can explore wonderful preparations such as this. The Rumi version has been on the menu for many years and is a mainstay on our catering menu because it works so well for large groups.

Serves 6–8

250 g (9 oz) cracked freekeh

2 tablespoons salt

1 bunch of flat-leaf parsley, roughly chopped

50 g (1¾ oz) Bulgarian feta, lightly crumbled

100 ml (3½ fl oz) Pomegranate dressing (page 46)

50 g (1¾ oz) fried almond flakes (see page 41), to serve

Wash the freekeh two or three times, then drain.

Place in a pot with the salt and 750 ml (3 cups) water and bring to the boil. Once it comes to the boil, simmer over a low heat until tender, then turn it off and let it sit for a further 3 minutes (see Note).

Strain the freekeh, then place in a bowl and let it cool to room temperature. Add the parsley, feta and pomegranate dressing and mix lightly but thoroughly. Be careful not to over mix; you don't want the feta to become a fine crumble and get lost in the grains. Garnish with the fried almond flakes.

Note
Different freekeh varieties will require different cooking times, so you may need to adjust accordingly. It will still be quite firm, but you don't want it to be crunchy. If using whole (not cracked) freekeh, soak for at least 2 hours before cooking.

COS AND HERB SALAD

It may come as a surprise that one of the dishes that I am most proud of at Rumi is our unique cos and herb salad. It is inspired by two Iranian traditions that I brought together in one bowl: the tradition of dipping cos leaves into Sekanjabin (a syrup of vinegar, sugar and mint; see page 28), and beginning a meal with a large plate of fresh herbs and radish. I thought it would be a stretch trying to get people to munch on whole herbs when we were not long out of an era where parsley was only thought of as a garnish, or chopped into oblivion and sprinkled on pasta (as I was taught to do in trade school), but happily, my customers loved it.

Serves 4

1 head of baby cos lettuce

25 g (½ cup) mint leaves

10 g (½ cup) flat-leaf parsley leaves

15 g (½ cup) coriander (cilantro) leaves

a few dill sprigs

salt flakes

70 ml (2¼ fl oz) Sweet-and-sour dressing (page 47)

2 radishes, sliced about 2 mm (¹⁄₁₆ in) thick

After washing and draining thoroughly, cut the cos into quarters lengthways and add to a mixing bowl with the herbs, a sprinkle of salt flakes and the well-shaken dressing. Toss, remove from the mixing bowl and arrange in a serving bowl or on a plate. Top with the sliced radish and another sprinkle of salt flakes.

Note
Don't forget to wash the herbs!
Try shredding the whole salad for a completely different texture.

Q. What if I don't like coriander (cilantro)? (Apparently 5 per cent of people say it tastes like soap.)
A. That's okay. You can leave the coriander out.

ICEBERG AND WALNUT TARATOOR

This salad is completely made up. Most importantly, it's really fresh and delicious. The crunchy, watery iceberg tempers the rich walnut taratoor perfectly.

Serves 6–8

1 × quantity Walnut taratoor (see below)

1 iceberg lettuce, cut into 10 cm (4 in) wide slices

1 × quantity Lemon dressing (page 46)

10 tarragon leaves

salt flakes

Walnut taratoor

1 teaspoon salt

10 g (¼ oz) Toum (page 34)

15 g (½ oz) tahini

1 tablespoon lemon juice

2 teaspoons extra-virgin olive oil

150 g (5½ oz) walnut halves

To make the taratoor, place all the ingredients, except for the walnuts, in a food processor with 100 ml (3½ fl oz) water. Pulse for a few seconds to combine then add half the walnuts and blend until smooth. Add the remaining walnuts and blend again until smooth. This will take a few minutes, with occasional pauses to scrape down the side. Check the consistency and add another 50 ml (1¾ fl oz) water if needed.

Spread the walnut taratoor on a plate and arrange the iceberg on top. Drizzle the lemon dressing over the dish and garnish with the tarragon and a sprinkle of salt flakes.

Note

If you find the taratoor a little thick, you can simply loosen it with more water.

Feel free to play around with the assembly. You could place the iceberg on the plate and dress with the sauce or even chop the lettuce into pieces.

A Fattoush for every Season

· Recipe pictured on page 123

Some of the first recipes that I wanted to include in this book were a series of fattoush that we change through the seasons at Rumi. Although there is a 'classic' Lebanese version, fattoush (as with panzanella) is a way to use up stale bread, so to me it made more sense to use salad ingredients at their best rather than obsessing about convention. The word 'fattoush' derives from the action of tearing the bread. I was delighted (and a little disappointed because I thought it was my own bright idea) when I opened Samin Nosrat's wonderful book Salt, Fat, Acid, Heat *and found that she took the same approach with her seasonal panzanella salads.*

Summer: Koussa fattoush

Koussa is the name for the white Lebanese zucchini (courgette) that are traditionally hollowed out and filled with rice and minced lamb. We use them here, barbecued, as the star of the salad.

Drain the chickpeas then place in a saucepan with plenty of cold water. Bring to the boil over a high heat, then reduce the heat to low and simmer for 1 hour, or until tender. Remove from the heat, stir in the salt, then leave to cool in the liquid.

While the chickpeas are cooling, preheat a charcoal barbecue. Cut the zucchini in half lengthways and place in a bowl. Add 2 tablespoons of the olive oil, season with salt and pepper and toss to coat well.

Chargrill the zucchini for 5 minutes on both sides, or until well caramelised, charred and soft in the centre. Transfer to a serving plate that has pictures of koussa painted on it and season with sea salt, then set aside.

Place the onion and tomatoes in a small bowl and gently squash the tomatoes – their juices will become part of the dressing. Add the drained chickpeas, lemon juice, parsley, mint and the remaining olive oil. Season with salt and toss to combine well, then adjust to taste – it may need a little more lemon, salt or oil.

To serve, season the yoghurt with a pinch of salt and the toum, and spoon over the zucchini. Add the fried bread and spoon the chickpea mixture over the top. Sprinkle with sumac and serve immediately.

Serves 4–6

50 g (1¾ oz) dried chickpeas, soaked overnight

1 teaspoon sea salt, plus extra to taste

800 g (1 lb 12 oz) white zucchini (courgette)

80 ml (⅓ cup) extra-virgin olive oil

⅓ red onion, very finely sliced

5 cherry tomatoes

juice of 1 lemon

½ bunch of flat-leaf parsley leaves, roughly chopped

10 mint leaves, torn

100 g (3½ oz) natural yoghurt

1 tablespoon Toum (page 34), or 2 finely crushed garlic cloves

2 flatbreads, cut into 3 cm (1¼ in) triangles and fried (see page 49)

ground sumac, for garnish and extra tang

Autumn: Tomato and shanklish fattoush

· Recipe pictured on page 122

Although tomatoes are a summer vegetable and such a wonderful summer memory for those of us who were lucky enough to have grown them at home, I find that the autumn glut of tomatoes are the sweetest and softest, and they work so well in this fattoush. Tomato, shanklish (a soft cheese made from yoghurt whey) and onion is a classic Lebanese combination, so I didn't just pull this one out of my hat.

Serves 4–6

2 large tomatoes, cored and cut into 5 cm (2 in) chunks

½ ball of shanklish cheese, crumbled

½ red onion, finely sliced

½ bunch of flat-leaf parsley leaves, roughly chopped

60 g (¼ cup) purslane

5 mint leaves, torn

2 flatbreads, cut into 3 cm (1¼ in) triangles and fried (see page 49)

1 teaspoon ground sumac, plus extra to serve

60 ml (¼ cup) Pomegranate dressing (page 46)

Place all the ingredients in a bowl, adding the dressing last, and mix. Serve on a platter or in a salad bowl that has pictures of tomatoes painted on it. Sprinkle with a little extra sumac for presentation.

Winter: Pumpkin and chickpea fattoush

· Recipe pictured on page 122

When the autumn tomatoes have run out and you're trying to write a new menu in Melbourne, you've gotta dig in. Thankfully, we always have pumpkin (squash). The inspiration for this combination came from one of the Moro (London) cookbooks during the time before the internet, when I would just stare at their books for hours. I can't even find the recipe now that I'm looking for it, but I just remember something to do with roasted cubes of pumpkin and lashings of tahini. The sweetness of the pumpkin works so well with the tahini. I added the dukkah and bread and turned it into a satisfying winter fattoush.

Drain the chickpeas then place in a saucepan with plenty of cold water. Bring to the boil over a high heat, then reduce the heat to low and simmer for 1 hour, or until tender. Remove from the heat, stir in the salt, then leave to cool in the liquid.

While the chickpeas are cooking, preheat your oven to 220°C (425°F).

Season the pumpkin with a pinch of salt and the olive oil. Spread on a baking tray and bake for about 20 minutes until cooked through. Alternatively, you could steam the pumpkin for around 10 minutes, then deep-fry it until dark brown.

When the chickpeas and pumpkin have cooled, place in a bowl with the remaining ingredients, adding the taratoor and lemon dressing last, and mix well.

Serve on a serving platter or in a salad bowl. Sprinkle with a little extra sumac for presentation.

Serves 4–6

50 g (1¾ oz) dried chickpeas, soaked overnight

1 teaspoon salt, plus extra to season the pumpkin

500 g (1 lb 2 oz) pumpkin (squash), cut into 5 cm (2 in) dice

1 tablespoon extra-virgin olive oil

½ bunch of flat-leaf parsley leaves, roughly chopped

1 tablespoon Dukkah (page 25)

2 flatbreads, cut into 3 cm (1¼ in) triangles and fried (see page 49)

1 teaspoon ground sumac, plus extra to serve

60 ml (¼ cup) Taratoor (page 42)

30 ml (1 fl oz) Lemon dressing (page 46)

Spring: Broad bean, asparagus and green almond fattoush

· Recipe pictured on page 123

Nothing announces spring to me more than these ingredients, and I love that they are at their absolute best during this period. This is a vibrant, fresh, crunchy salad that makes a refreshing addition to a full spread or a meal in its own right. I was honoured to have served this when I was a guest at Tawlet restaurant in Beirut. I made this up all by myself. Aren't I clever?

Serves 4–6

40 g (¼ cup) peas (podded weight)

185 g (1 cup) broad beans (podded weight)

1 tablespoon extra-virgin olive oil

1 bunch of asparagus, cut into 2 cm (¾ in) lengths

1 avocado, peeled and stone removed

100 g (3½ oz) Taratoor (page 42)

½ bunch of flat-leaf parsley leaves, roughly chopped

¼ bunch of watercress, sprigs picked

10 mint leaves, torn

10 broad bean leaves, torn

2 flatbreads, cut into 3 cm (1¼ in) triangles and fried (see page 49)

1 teaspoon ground sumac, plus extra to serve

50 ml (1¾ fl oz) Lemon dressing (page 46)

3 green almonds, finely sliced

Fill two small bowls with cold water and ice and set aside.

Fill a small pot with heavily salted water and bring to the boil over a high heat. Add the peas to the pot and boil for 1 minute before removing with a slotted spoon and placing in the iced water. Drain once cold.

Bring the water back to the boil then add the broad beans. Boil for 3 minutes then remove and place the broad beans in the second bowl of iced water. When cold, drain and remove the loose light-green skins to reveal the vibrant green centre of the broad bean. Discard the skin.

Heat the oil in a pan over a medium heat for about 30 seconds before adding the asparagus and sautéing for about 2 minutes.

Make an avocado dressing by puréeing the avocado and taratoor in a food processor until smooth.

Place all the ingredients in a bowl, adding the dressings last, and mix well. Serve on a serving platter or in a salad bowl. Scatter over the green almonds and sprinkle with a little extra sumac for presentation.

Q. Can I use frozen peas and broad beans instead?
A. Absolutely. This eliminates the steps of podding them. Simply run the frozen peas and beans under hot water to defrost them. Just be sure to remove the loose skins from the broad beans before using.

Clockwise from top-left: Winter: Pumpkin and chickpea fattoush (page 120); Summer: Koussa fattoush (page 118); Spring: Broad bean, asparagus and green almond fattoush (page 121); Autumn: Tomato and shanklish fattoush (page 119)

BROCCOLI TABBOULEH

You say tabouli, I say tabbouleh.

If there's one recipe I suggest you take from this book and share with your family and friends, it's this one. It is inspired by my wife Nat's raw broccoli salad, which is a regular feature of our family table. I came up with this recipe on one of the rare occasions I was making dinner for the kids (while Nat was mayor of the local city council). Looking for inspiration that would do her proud and not be outright rejected by the kids, I found some broccoli in the fridge and thought I'd have a go at her salad, which normally contains chopped raw broccoli, toasted almonds and pepitas (pumpkin seeds), and Persian feta. Instead, somehow, I made a connection between the texture of raw broccoli and the texture of burghul, which is an integral ingredient in tabbouleh. Broccoli tabbouleh was born. And it's gluten free! I think I'm pretty clever with this one.

Trim the broccoli of the fibrous end, then chop the tender stem and florets as finely as you can.

Place all the ingredients in a bowl and mix together. Be sure that everything is well coated with the lemon juice and olive oil. I would suggest leaving it for 5 minutes after mixing then coming back to it with any adjustments to the seasoning – it should be juicy and salty!

Serves 8

1 large head of broccoli

2 ripe tomatoes, cut into 5 mm (¼ in) dice

1 bunch of flat-leaf parsley, leaves picked then finely chopped

¼ bunch of mint, leaves picked then shredded

75 ml (⅓ cup) lemon juice

150 ml (5 fl oz) extra-virgin olive oil

1 teaspoon Lebanese 7 spice

2 spring onions (scallions), finely sliced

½ teaspoon salt

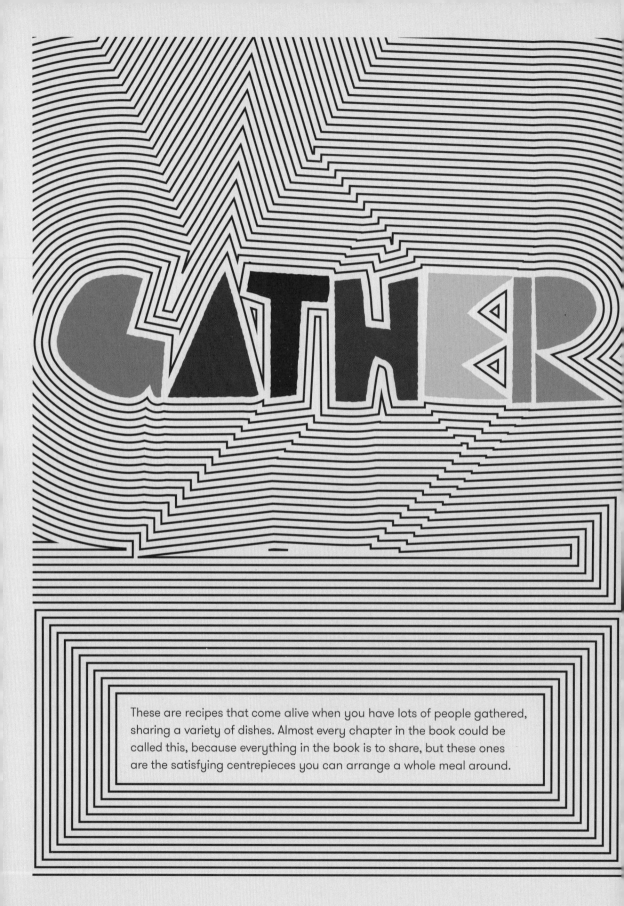

GATHER

These are recipes that come alive when you have lots of people gathered, sharing a variety of dishes. Almost every chapter in the book could be called this, because everything in the book is to share, but these ones are the satisfying centrepieces you can arrange a whole meal around.

LAMB SHOULDER

This dish has been a crowd pleaser at Rumi since we first added it to the menu over ten years ago. We serve it with Sekanjabin (page 28), which is, ultimately, a mint sauce. Surprisingly frequently we have gruff older men come up to the kitchen with their daughters (who have nervously brought them to Rumi) and say 'Oh maaate, that lamb, I don't know what you do to it but ... '.

This is a very simple recipe that should be started the day before. These quantities are just a guide. You could buy 500 g (1 lb 2 oz) for two people, or scale up to a whole forequarter for a feast.

Rub the lamb shoulder with the advieh and salt and leave in the fridge for the flavours to penetrate the meat – preferably overnight, but an hour or two is okay.

About 6 hours before you plan to serve the meal, preheat the oven to 140°C (275°F). Place the rubbed meat, skin side up, in a roasting tin that is not much bigger than the lamb so that it fits snugly. Cover with a sheet of baking paper then a sheet of foil. Fold the foil over the edges of the tin tightly so any steam will be trapped during the cooking process.

Slow-roast for about 6 hours. Check after 5½ hours by pushing the meat to see if it falls away from the bone. If it is still firm, give it another 30 minutes. Once the lamb is soft and falling away from the bone, remove the foil and baking paper, increase the heat to 250°C (480°F) and cook for a further 30 minutes, uncovered, to dry out the spice crust.

If you prefer, you can cook your lamb shoulder in a Dutch oven. Place the rubbed meat in the casserole and cover with the lid. Slow-roast for 6 hours, removing the lid for the last 30 minutes of cooking time.

TO SERVE, OFFER THE LAMB WITH ANY OF THE FOLLOWING:

Sekanjabin (pictured opposite, page 28)
Green taratoor and Red taratoor (page 43)
Harissa (page 36)
Labne (page 31)
Muhammara (page 37)
Spiced salts (page 25)
Tahini yoghurt (page 31)
Taratoor (page 42)
Toum (page 34)

Serves 4

1–2 kg (2 lb 4 oz–4 lb 8 oz) bone-in lamb shoulder
100 g (3½ oz) Advieh (page 24)
20 g (¾ oz) salt

Q. What part of the shoulder can I use?
A. Any part is fine. If you like a lot of fat, ask your butcher to include the ribs, and if you prefer big chunks of meat, ask for the shoulder only, but make sure the bone is kept in.

Q. Can you use any other cut of lamb?
A. You could use lamb shanks instead of lamb shoulder, one shank per person. Reduce the cooking time to 2½–3 hours.

Q. Can I prepare any part in advance?
A. You can cook the meat days in advance then reheat it, covered, at about 100°C (200°F) with 250 ml (1 cup) water in the bottom of the tin until the meat has softened and warmed up. This can take about 1 hour.

Q. What if I can't find advieh?
A. If you are not using the advieh in this book (see page 24), use garam masala or any spice mix that comes from the east or south of the Mediterranean, such as Baharat (page 24) or ras el hanout.

RUMI MEATBALLS

These meatballs have been on the menu since the day we opened and are inspired by the Persian recipe kofte tabrizi, which is a giant meatball that is stuffed with eggs, onions and dried fruit. This version takes inspiration from the meat/rice combination that makes the meatballs beautifully delicate. They are great for kids, too, as my son Patrick will attest by eating a whole serve to himself and then his brother's leftovers.

Bring the rice to the boil in a saucepan of water set over a high heat and boil until only just cooked. Drain, then chill. (This can be done the day before.)

To make the meatballs, place all the ingredients in a large bowl, ensuring that your rice is also cold, and mix vigorously until well combined.

Divide the mixture into pieces approximately 50 g (1¾ oz) each. Roll into neat balls and refrigerate until the sauce is ready.

Now, make the sauce in a wide-based pan large enough to eventually accommodate the meatballs in one to two layers.

Sweat the onion in the olive oil for about 10 minutes over a low heat. This is a very important step as you want to draw the sweetness out of the onion. The onion should be translucent.

Add the tomatoes, bring to the boil, then reduce the heat to medium–low and cook for a further 30 minutes. Stir in the salt, then add 125 ml (½ cup) water and bring back to a simmer.

Gently drop the meatballs into the sauce, ensuring they all sink down well, and monitor until it returns to the boil. Turn the heat down to a very low simmer and cook for another 30 minutes.

Serves 6–8, or makes 18 meatballs

Meatballs
110 g (½ cup) medium-grain rice

1 small onion, grated or minced in a food processor

500 g (1 lb 2 oz) minced (ground) lamb

1 egg

½ bunch of flat-leaf parsley, finely chopped

1 teaspoon Advieh (page 24)

2 teaspoons salt

1 teaspoon Saffron water (page 47)

Sauce
1 onion, finely diced

100 ml (3½ fl oz) extra-virgin olive oil

1 kg (2 lb 4 oz) tinned chopped tomatoes

2 teaspoons salt

Note
These go nicely with a dollop of Labne (page 31).

TAHINI CHICKEN

This is a dish that I can't believe is not more commonplace. It is basically a chicken version of the classic Lebanese baked fish dish, samke harra. In this recipe the chicken is smothered in Taratoor (page 42) and finished with various nuts, parsley and chilli. This version is made with roasted chicken, but you could steam, bake or poach the chicken, too.

Serves 4–8

1 × free-range chicken

1 tablespoon vegetable oil

1 tablespoon salt

1 teaspoon Baharat (page 24)

1 × quantity Taratoor
  (page 42)

50 g (1¾ oz) fried almonds
  (see page 41)

1 tablespoon fried pine nuts
  (see page 41)

50 g (1¾ oz) walnuts, chopped

½ bunch of flat-leaf parsley,
  shredded

1 tablespoon ground sumac

1 teaspoon Turkish chilli
  powder

Remove the chicken from the fridge about 20 minutes before you want to cook it and preheat your oven to 220°C (425°F).

Rub the vegetable oil all over the chicken then season with the salt and baharat. Place in a roasting tin and cook for approximately 1 hour and 20 minutes. To check that your chicken is cooked, pierce the thigh with a knife – the juices should be clear. Remove from the oven and allow to rest for about 20 minutes before carving. Lower the oven temperature to 180°C (350°F).

Take the bird apart by removing the legs and cutting them into thighs and drumsticks. Remove the breasts from the bone and cut each breast into two or three pieces. Pick the rest of the meat off the carcass and add to the pile of chicken pieces. Drain the fat and excess juices out of the tray and set aside (see Note). Place the cut chicken in the tray and pour the taratoor over it. Return to the oven for 5 minutes. Serve on your platter of choice topped with the mixed nuts, parsley, sumac and Turkish chilli.

Note
After draining most of the fat away from the juices (and discarding it), you could warm the remaining pan juices and drizzle over the chicken before serving.
  As with the fish in the tahini brandade recipe (see page 138), the leftovers can be shredded and served with crispy bread or used to make an excellent sandwich filling.

EGGPLANT M'NAZLEH

As I wrote this book, I became aware of just how much my mother's cooking had influenced me through osmosis, even though we never cooked together. Eggplant (aubergine) m'nazleh makes an appearance mostly during Lent, when many Lebanese Christians abstain from meat and dairy products. This is the one recipe that has found its way onto the Rumi menu that is truly my mother's recipe. Well, as close to it as possible. We try.

This dish can be served hot but is most often eaten at room temperature. You can leave the peeled eggplant whole or cut in half for a more elegant presentation.

Fry the garlic and chilli in the olive oil until fragrant, but don't allow it to colour. Add the onion, cover and sweat over a low heat until very soft, stirring occasionally.

Add the capsicum and salt and cook, covered, till very soft, about 30 minutes.

Add the tomatoes and bring to the boil. Don't forget to stir all the way to the bottom of the pot to prevent it sticking. Reduce the heat, cover, and simmer for 2 hours, or until the tomato has broken down and the oil has separated.

Stir in the baharat and check the seasoning.

Heat 2 cm (¾ in) oil in a frying pan and fry the eggplant until brown all over. Better still, use a deep-fryer (see page 49). Drain in a colander and season with a pinch of salt. Leave in the colander for around 10 minutes to allow any excess oil to drain away. Add to the sauce and simmer until the eggplant is very soft.

Serves 4

2 garlic cloves, thinly sliced

1 red chilli, deseeded and finely sliced

1 green chilli, deseeded and finely sliced

200 ml (7 fl oz) extra-virgin olive oil

1 onion, cut into 3 cm (1¼ in) strips

1 green capsicum (pepper), cut into 5 cm (2 in) pieces

1 teaspoon salt

1 × 400 g (14 oz) tin chopped tomatoes

½ teaspoon Baharat (page 24)

2 eggplants (aubergines), peeled and cut into large chunks about the size of a golf ball

THE QUAIL THAT ANTHONY BOURDAIN ATE

One of the most memorable moments in our history is when Matt Preston brought in Anthony Bourdain to film No Reservations. We were asked to feed Anthony whatever we liked, and this was one of the dishes he ate. The highest form of compliment came when he ordered another plate – 'more birdy'. He loved it!

It is a combination inspired by Iranian flavours: saffron and onion in the marinade and the Iranian verjuice dressing. I recommend lighting a charcoal barbecue for this one, but of course you can cook it over a gas barbecue, too.

Serves 6–12

150 ml (5 fl oz) grape
  molasses
300 ml (10½ fl oz) verjuice
6 jumbo quails, butterflied by
  your butcher
salt, to season
½ teaspoon ground ginger
½ teaspoon ground black
  pepper
1 teaspoon Saffron water
  (page 47)
1 tablespoon onion juice
  (see Note)

Make the dressing by adding the grape molasses and verjuice to a bottle or jar, seal and shake vigorously for 5–10 seconds. Set aside.

The quails can be separated into legs and breasts, or kept in one piece. Place in a bowl with the spices, saffron water and onion juice and leave to marinate for at least 4 hours for the best results. Season the skin side with salt just before cooking.

To cook, heat a charcoal barbecue grill to high and cook the quail, skin side down, for 3 minutes. Turn and cook for another 3 minutes. The breast can be a little pink, but the legs should be well cooked.

Take off the grill, place on a serving plate, skin side up, and drizzle with the dressing.

Note
If you're separating the quails into legs and breasts, you may like to skewer them into quail 'kebabs' after marinating.

To make the onion juice, blend two peeled onions in a food processor, then pass the onion pulp through a piece of muslin cloth.

TAHINI 'BRANDADE'

Put simply, brandade is a classic French fish preparation of 'creamed or puréed' fish. Tahini has a way of creating the sort of creaminess that would otherwise be created using animal fats or emulsions. I noticed that at the end of a lunch where Mum had made tahini fish (samke harra), she would dish up the remainder for all of us to take home, by which stage the fish had been basically mashed. I found that it was delicious to eat cold with flatbread rather than with a fork. I can't remember the exact circumstances of how my dish came to be, but I remember needing to cook quite a lot of fish in a hurry and had to do something with it. I baked the fish, mashed it and folded through the tahini – it was perfect. This recipe can be prepared a few days before you need it, but be sure to allow it to come to room temperature before serving.

Preheat your oven to 200°C (400°F).

Line a baking tray with baking paper and brush it with a little olive oil.

Lay the fillets on the tray, skin side down, then sprinkle the flesh with salt. Bake for approximately 6 minutes. The fish will be ready when the flesh flakes easily when pressed. (If you're nervous about undercooked fish you can leave it a little longer as this recipe can handle it.) Set aside to cool. When cool, pull the flesh away from the skin and shred into a bowl. Add the taratoor and toum and mix well.

Arrange on a plate or in a bowl, then drizzle with the olive oil. Sprinkle with the chilli and sumac.

If using the flaked almonds, you could simply sprinkle them on top or get pretty corny and stick them into the brandade to look like fish scales. You could even use pine nuts for eyes.

Serves 4–6

500 g (1 lb 2 oz) white fish fillets, such as snapper or trevally

salt, to season

100 g (3½ oz) Taratoor (page 42)

20 g (¾ oz) Toum (page 34)

2 tablespoons extra-virgin olive oil, plus extra for brushing

1 teaspoon Turkish chilli powder

1 teaspoon ground sumac

1 tablespoon toasted flaked almonds (optional; see page 41)

Note
If the fish has been in the fridge, it may benefit from another drizzle of taratoor and a pinch of salt stirred through to loosen it all up.

You could serve this with crisp Lebanese flatbread or some sourdough toast. I recommend serving alongside some pickles, too (see page 72).

SLOW-COOKED VEG

Slow-cooked vegetables, not overcooked vegetables. The difference? Intent. When you choose to cook vegetables beyond that desirable al dente vibrancy typical of Asian dishes or contemporary European cooking, they are treated in a different way. Compared with steamed or wok-tossed vegetables, Middle Eastern vegetable dishes are usually cooked for a lot longer, achieving a deeply satisfying and rich flavour that has given the region its reputation for having great vegetable dishes. They can be standalone dishes, but can also make a great meal when presented as part of a broader spread or paired with roast meats or baked fish.

This recipe uses green beans, but they can be substituted with fennel, broad beans and leeks, or even lettuce such as cos or endive.

Place the onion and oil in a saucepan that will easily fit all of your chosen vegetables. The gentle cooking of the onion is a crucial part of getting the depth of flavour into these dishes.

Cook the onion over a medium heat until it is just about to change from translucent to light brown. This will take about 20 minutes.

In the meantime, blanch or steam the beans for a minute or two. Drain and add to the pan with the onion.

Add the tomatoes and increase the heat till all the ingredients are steaming. Reduce the heat to low, cover and cook for 30 minutes.

Stir in the spices and season with salt to taste. If you intend to serve these cold, then only season a little and adjust the seasoning when cold.

Serves 8

600 g (1 lb 5 oz) diced onion
400 ml (14 fl oz) olive oil
1 kg (2 lb 4 oz) green beans
100 g (3½ oz) tinned or fresh chopped tomatoes
1 flat tablespoon Baharat (page 24)
1 tablespoon ground black pepper
salt, to taste

Note
You can leave the tomato out of this recipe; many versions of these dishes are cooked with oil only.

These are great eaten at room temperature or cold and will keep in the fridge for 4–5 days.

FISH KEBABS WITH CASPIAN OLIVE AND WALNUT SAUCE

You can use any firm-fleshed, chunky white fish for these kebabs, but my first choice would be Murray cod. It's been an iconic Australian fish for a long time, but only in recent years has the farmed variety given Murray cod a more regular spot at the table. Its fat content and structure hold up particularly well on the barbecue, and its sustainability credentials are championed by its new farmers. I've paired it here with an olive and walnut sauce which has its origins in the mountainous region of northern Iran on the southern coast of the Caspian Sea. A fun fact that may interest you is that this area of Iran gets twice the annual rainfall of London. Add that to your image of Iran.

Cut the fish fillet into pieces about 3 × 3 cm (1¼ × 1¼ in). Place in a bowl and coat in the oil and advieh. Thread onto a skewer with the skin side of each cube facing the same direction.

To make the sauce, place the walnuts in a food processor and pulse a few times until they are chopped into pea-sized pieces. Remove from the food processor and place in a mixing bowl.

Add the pitted olives to the food processor and blend to a paste – it doesn't have to be very smooth. Remove from the food processor and add to the bowl with the walnuts.

Add the lemon, verjuice and pomegranate molasses to the bowl and mix until well combined. Add the olive oil and mix well. Add the parsley and mint and stir through. Season with the black pepper. It shouldn't need salt as the olives are normally salty.

Take the fish skewers, season with salt and place, skin side down, on a hot grill for 3–4 minutes to allow the skin to crisp. Turn and cook for a further minute or two until the flesh turns white.

Place the skewers on a serving plate and drizzle the sauce over the top. You could finish with a drizzle of olive oil or Lemon dressing (page 46).

Serves 6

500 g (1 lb 2 oz) chunky, firm-fleshed white fish fillets, such as Murray cod or swordfish, skin on

50 ml (1¾ fl oz) extra-virgin olive oil, plus extra to serve (optional)

1 teaspoon Advieh (page 24)

salt, to season

Olive and walnut sauce

40 g (1½ oz) walnuts

100 g (3½ oz) pitted green olives

200 ml (7 fl oz) lemon juice

200 ml (7 fl oz) verjuice

100 ml (3½ fl oz) pomegranate molasses

200 ml (7 fl oz) extra-virgin olive oil

½ bunch of flat-leaf parsley, finely shredded

6 mint sprigs, leaves picked and finely shredded

2 teaspoons ground black pepper

Q. Do I have to barbecue the fish?
A. No, you can leave the fillets whole and pan-fry them instead, but be sure to start with the skin side down to make it crispy, unless using skinless fillets.

Barbecue

· Recipe pictured on page 146-7

What to say about barbecue? I have trouble romanticising barbecue as it is literally the oldest form of cooking, shared by every culture on earth. In my own family, there are rituals that come with barbecuing, like my father following the exact same routine every time the extended family gathers for a Sunday barbecue. He prepares the charcoal pit with an old cut-up beer keg filled with kindling and a wax box waiting for Mum to give the word to light the coals, then my wife Nat pushes him out of the way to take over. This is just a part of my story, and I'm not here to rewrite your barbecue story because I think that everyone has their own rituals. But I am hoping that the tips I share with you will make your barbecuing better, whether it's inspiring you to cook on charcoal, or marinating your meat beforehand, or to just use more salt. Maybe reimagine those boring barbecued lamb chops, or add a little Toum (page 34) to your chicken skewers – and don't forget to burn your eggplants (aubergines) on the coals when you're finished grilling!

THE GRILL

It's the idea of lighting some charcoal to cook on that's most exciting, whichever type of grill you use. You really just need a few bricks, a mesh grill, charcoal and some skewers. Another option is a metal box on legs, and you can normally find these at Middle Eastern shops. Or you could step it up to a Japanese hibachi-style grill, which is great for skewers and holds its heat really well. I don't think this is the book to discover which charcoal is best (maybe check its sustainability credentials) or methods for lighting it, but one big tip is to light the charcoal about an hour before you need it. I recommend this for a couple of reasons. Firstly, and most importantly, if you're having trouble lighting it, like I often do, you've got enough time to resurrect things before your best mate comes over offering all the advice that nobody needs when you're trying to get a fire going. Secondly, it allows the coals time to be fully alight, then settle a little before you start grilling. This gives you a more even heat and helps reduce the crazy flare-ups that we all know turn your chops into 'those' chops.

WHAT TO GRILL

Lamb cutlets or chops seemed to be top of the poll (of four people) that I ran, followed by chicken skewers. Both of these are also very popular on the Middle Eastern barbecue. Just be sure to marinate them for at least 2 hours before cooking. Sausages rank highly, but rather than the same sausages you've been cooking for years, maybe seek out some Lebanese

Lamb cutlets, ribs or chops

1 kg (2 lb 4 oz) lamb cutlets, ribs or chops

1 onion, very finely minced, or use the juice by squeezing the minced onion through a cloth

1 tablespoon extra-virgin olive oil

½ teaspoon salt, plus extra for cooking

1 teaspoon Baharat (page 24)

Toum (page 34), for brushing after cooking

za'atar, to season

Chicken skewers, wings or steaks

1 kg (2 lb 4 oz) chicken pieces, wings or steaks

1 onion, very finely minced, or use the juice by squeezing the minced onion through a cloth

1 tablespoon extra-virgin olive oil

½ teaspoon salt, plus extra for cooking

pinch of sweet paprika

Toum (page 34), for brushing after cooking

Turkish chilli powder, to season, or Muhammara (page 37), to coat

Asparagus, corn on the cob, thickly sliced potatoes, halved baby onions

extra-virgin olive oil, for brushing

salt

Toum (page 34), za'atar, Muhammara (page 37), Turkish chilli powder, Red taratoor (page 43), Green taratoor (page 43) or Taratoor (page 42), to brush or toss to coat

Seafood, whole fish or fillets, skewers

salt

extra-virgin olive oil and Advieh (page 24), to marinate

Red taratoor (page 43), Green taratoor (page 43), Taratoor (page 42), Muhammara (page 37), harissa, or Fennel salt (page 25), to brush or coat

ma'anek or Turkish sujuk. Chicken wings are delicious, especially when you cook them for a long time to give them a little charring. Less common on the barbecue is fish, which works perfectly well. Whole fish are great as they're exciting, and being on the bone keeps them moist and allows a margin of error if you overcook them. Whole snapper straight on the grill works perfectly, but you could try skewering chunks of a bigger fish. Least common of all are vegetables, which I believe are a treat to barbecue. Whether it's corn on the cob or in-season asparagus, the char you get from the grill pairs very well with Middle Eastern condiments.

If you've got your barbecue going early, allowing it to settle a little, you should be able to cook the smaller meats and vegetables while the fire is at its hottest. Then, as the coals settle further, you can cook your bigger things, so that they become well charred but cooked all the way through. For example, you want to cook a whole snapper on a gentler heat to ensure it gets a good char but cooks all the way through. If you put it on when the fire is really hot, it will be black on the outside and raw in the middle.

MARINADES

Marinades aren't as common as you may think for Lebanese barbecue, but they impart extra flavour into your grilled foods and can also be used to tenderise meats. A common Iranian method is to use grated onion, which also adds a little sweetness. Of course, you can follow recipes to the letter, or you can use what you have on hand and not worry about going out to find that one spice that you're missing. But if you do want to add a little kick, Baharat (page 24) is a great all-rounder. Also, let this serve as a reminder that it is your food, so if you don't like chilli, for example, just leave it out. Always add a little salt to the marinade, and salt again just before grilling – enough to be condemned by the Heart Foundation. As my son said to me at a recent Sunday barbecue, Tayta (his grandmother) sure knows how to use salt.

CONDIMENTS

If you took my advice and made a whole lot of recipes from the first chapter, you will be spoilt for choice: chicken and Muhammara (page 37), lamb with Toum (page 34) and za'atar, asparagus and Taratoor (page 42), fish Mint butter (page 28).

SALADS

The best salads for barbecue need to be fresh and tart. You've probably become an expert at my Broccoli tabbouleh (page 124), so be sure to make some of that as well as the Iceberg and walnut taratoor (page 116).

Clockwise from top-left:
Chicken wings (see page 144),
Onions (see page 145),
Whole fish (see page 145),
Corn (see page 145),
Prawns (see page 145),
Lamb chops (see page 144),
Chicken thighs (see page 144)

CIRCASSIAN CHICKEN

This dish is a version of the traditional Turkish dish made from shredded chicken, walnuts and paprika. Here, poached chicken is folded through Muhammara (page 37).

Circassian chicken should be served warm or at room temperature, not cold from the fridge.

Serves 4–6

2 skinless chicken breasts
500 ml (2 cups) chicken stock, or salted water with 1 quartered onion
160 g (5¾ oz) Muhammara (page 37)

Optional garnishes
10 walnut halves, roughly chopped
2 tablespoons Salça butter (page 28)
sprinkle of Turkish chilli powder
sprinkle of nigella seeds

Note
You could brine your chicken in leftover pickling liquid (see page 72) the night before you start cooking this dish. Discard the pickling liquid before you poach the chicken.

If you have some steamed or leftover roast chicken, use it instead of the poached chicken.

If you find the muhammara too rich for this particular preparation, or you are scraping the bottom of your jar, you can dilute it with a little of the poaching liquid or some warm water.

You could serve this dish with crisp Lebanese flatbread (see page 49) or some sourdough toast.

I recommend serving alongside some pickles (see page 72).

Place the chicken in a saucepan with the cold chicken stock or salted water (with the onion) and bring to the boil over a high heat. Reduce the heat to low and poach, uncovered, for approximately 15 minutes until just cooked. Remove the chicken from the liquid and let it cool.

When it is cool enough to handle, shred the chicken and place in a bowl. Add the muhammara and mix well. Spread on a plate or place in a bowl and top with one or all of the optional garnishes.

THREE HOT YOGHURT SOUPS

Hot yoghurt soups are little known outside of Levantine homes, but are the base for some of the most heart-warming dishes. One of my favourites is my mum's shish barak, which is a soup containing little tortellini-shaped dumplings filled with minced lamb. You rarely find it in restaurants.

The first of these recipes is a variation of Mum's shish barak yoghurt soup. Mine is made with chicken and pistachio. The second recipe is a yoghurt noodle soup inspired by the Iranian noodle soup, ash reshteh. The third, laban immo, is a much-loved dish of braised meat in yoghurt sauce.

Soup base

Whisk the egg yolks and yoghurt in a bowl with the salt.

In another bowl mix the cornflour thoroughly with 2 tablespoons water, then add to the yoghurt mix. You can use this base to create any of the three meals below.

Serves 10

2 egg yolks

1 kg (2 lb 4 oz) full-cream yoghurt (preferably home-made; see page 30)

1 teaspoon salt

10 g (¼ oz) cornflour (cornstarch)

Shish barak yoghurt soup

· Recipe pictured on page 154

This soup was rated one of the top ten dishes of the year by The Age when it was on the menu at Rumi. It really comes together when you combine the three elements: cooked rice, shish barak and the soup base. As much as it is great to make it from scratch, because most of the work is in the shish barak, if you don't have the time or commitment to make your own dumplings you easily use ready-made dumplings. Simply add them to the yoghurt soup base with the cooked rice.

Serves 10

20 g (¾ oz) medium-grain rice

200 g (1½ cups) plain (all-purpose) flour

200 g (7 oz) minced (ground) chicken

½ small onion, finely chopped

1 tablespoon pistachio kernels, roughly chopped

1 teaspoon Lebanese 7 spice

½ teaspoon dried mint

1 teaspoon salt

1 × quantity Soup base (see opposite)

Q. Can store-bought pastry work for the dumplings?
A. I have found that gyoza (not wonton) pastry works really well, and it's easy to find at Asian grocers. Easier still would be to buy the dumplings already made. Turkish mante work best, but if you really want to try this soup and can't find mante, try tortellini.

Q. Do I have to use minced (ground) chicken?
A. You can use any mince for this recipe, so if you have some spare minced (ground) lamb or beef around just follow the recipe with your choice of meat. Traditionally it is done with lamb and no pistachio, so feel free to experiment.

Boil the rice in salted water for approximately 20 minutes, or until cooked through. Drain and set aside.

To make the dough for the shish barak, place the flour in a bowl with a pinch of salt and gradually add 100 ml (3½ fl oz) water until the mixture comes together. Knead gently until the dough no longer sticks to your hands. Set aside, covered, for at least 30 minutes. If you want to, feel free to use a mixer fitted with a dough hook for this step.

Place the chicken mince, onion, pistachio, 7 spice, half the dried mint and the salt in a bowl and mix until well combined.

Now we make the discs of dough that will hold the chicken mixture. Cut off a piece of dough about the size of a tennis ball or a little smaller. Roll into a long, skinny log shape the thickness of your thumb. Cut the log into pieces about 2 cm (¾ in) long. Take a piece of dough and press it between your finger and thumb, turning as you go, until it has stretched out to around 3 cm (1¼ in) in diameter. It will be about 2 mm (⅟₁₆ in) thick. You can use a rolling pin on a lightly floured board, but it's more fun squeezing the discs into shape. Repeat till you have used all the dough.

Place a flat teaspoon of the chicken mix on each disc. Fold the disc over to meet the other side and become a half-moon. Rub a little water on the inside edge and press down to seal. You can stop at this point if it's getting too much or, if you are loving the process, keep going and make the traditional shape, which is like a tortellini. Do this by bringing the two points of the half-moon across the long edge as if the shish barak is reaching out its arms and hugging itself. Again, use a little water to stick the points together. Refrigerate until ready to cook.

Place the soup base and cooked rice in a saucepan set over a medium heat and stir often as it comes to the boil. Once boiling, increase the heat a little, add 500 ml (2 cups) water, bring back to a simmer, then slowly add the shish barak. Once all the shish barak are in, give the soup a gentle stir and bring it back to the boil. Once boiling, reduce the heat and simmer gently for about 10 minutes until the dumplings are cooked. Serve in your favourite soup bowls and garnish with the remaining dried mint.

Yoghurt noodle soup

• Recipe pictured on page 155

This soup is really hearty and can be a meal in its own right.

All the elements of this dish can be prepared up to a couple of days before then put together when needed. The onion, in particular, will benefit from being prepared well in advance to let the flavours develop.

To cook the dried chickpeas, you'll first need to soak them overnight with a pinch of bicarbonate of soda (baking soda). The following day, drain and rinse them, then place in a saucepan and fill with water equal to three times the depth of the chickpeas. Bring to the boil, then simmer gently for 30–40 minutes, or until tender. Turn off the heat and add 1 teaspoon of the salt. Leave the chickpeas in the water to cool. Before you start to assemble the soup, drain the chickpeas and set aside.

To cook the lentils, add them to a saucepan and fill with water equal to three times the depth of the lentils. Add the remaining salt, bring to the boil, then reduce the heat and simmer gently for about 20 minutes until tender. Leave the lentils in the water to cool. Before you start to assemble the soup, drain the lentils and set aside.

Cook the noodles according to the packet instructions in plenty of salted boiling water.

Heat the vegetable oil in a saucepan and, once hot, add the onion. Cook over a high heat, stirring regularly, until it begins to colour. Turn the heat down to very low and continue cooking until the onion is very dark brown and beginning to crisp. Add the turmeric and dried mint and cook for another 30 seconds. Remove from the heat, allow the onion to cool slightly, then stir in the olive oil.

To serve, place the soup base in a saucepan set over a medium heat and stir often until it comes to the boil. Turn the heat up a little then add the drained chickpeas and lentils. Stir gently until it comes back to the boil, then add the noodles and bring back to the boil again. Stir again and reduce to a gentle simmer for a couple of minutes, then remove from the heat.

Serve in your favourite soup bowls and garnish with the oily turmeric onion.

Serves 4–6

50 g (1¾ oz) dried chickpeas

pinch of bicarbonate of soda (baking soda)

2 teaspoons salt

50 g (½ cup) green, brown or puy lentils

100 g (3½ oz) Iranian soup noodles (see Note)

1 tablespoon vegetable oil

1 onion, sliced into crescents about 2 mm (¹⁄₁₆ in) thick

½ teaspoon ground turmeric

½ teaspoon dried mint

100 ml (3½ fl oz) extra-virgin olive oil

1 × quantity Soup base (page 150)

Note
I like my chickpeas soft, so I leave them to cook a bit longer because they harden a little as they cool.

When the chickpeas are simmering, they may produce a foam that will float to the top. This can be skimmed and discarded. Similarly, the skins may float to the top, and these can be discarded or not, according to your taste.

If you can't find Iranian soup noodles, you can use your favourite pasta. Spaghetti or linguine work well.

Laban immo

·Recipe pictured on page 155

This is not a dish that we had growing up but I couldn't resist it once I discovered it. It's traditionally cooked with boned lamb shanks, but I use a cut of veal nicknamed the 'bell' by one of our butchers, Leo Donati of Donati's Meats in Lygon Street, Carlton. I can never get a straight answer out of Leo when I ask what the cut is technically called, but it's a delicious nugget of meat from somewhere in the leg.

Serves 4–6

500 g (1 lb 2 oz) veal 'bells' or lamb shanks

2 onions, peeled and quartered

1 teaspoon green cardamom pods

1 bay leaf

10 black peppercorns

1 cinnamon stick

100 g (3½ oz) medium-grain rice

½ × quantity Soup base (page 150)

50 g (⅓ cup) peas

20 g (¾ oz) fried almonds (see page 41)

20 g (¾ oz) Mint butter (page 28), melted

Note

You'll notice that this is not so much a soup as a sauce, generously smothering the meat. You can use any cut of braising meat you are comfortable with. Lamb shanks are obviously great, but lamb shoulder or diced braising steak works fine, too. It's just not as pretty. The meat can be cooked days in advance and refrigerated for when you need it.

For a heartier meal, consider adding some carrots and potatoes. You can add these vegetables to the poaching stock till they are cooked to your liking then remove and set aside, to be added during the final assembly process.

Start by preparing a stock to poach the veal in. You can use meat stock (if you have some handy), whey (from making labne, see page 31) or water. If using water, add 1 tablespoon salt. This stock will have no further use once you have finished poaching the veal.

Combine the onion, spices and veal in a large saucepan, then add enough poaching stock to cover the veal by double its height.

Bring to the boil then lower to a simmer. As the foam and excess fat rises to the surface it will need to be skimmed and discarded. Regulate your heat to the point at which the meat is barely simmering and cook until it is very soft and melting. This will take 2–3 hours, depending on your cut of meat. Once cooked, allow to sit in the liquid till cool enough to handle. Check the meat for any excess sinew or fat that can be easily removed. If using shanks, remove the bone. Set the meat aside and discard the stock.

Boil the rice in salted water for approximately 20 minutes, or until cooked through. Drain and set aside.

To serve, place the soup base in a saucepan set over a medium heat and stir often until the soup starts to boil. At this stage you can turn it up a little then add the meat, the cooked rice and the peas. Stir gently until the soup boils again, then reduce to a gentle simmer till the peas are cooked then remove from the heat.

Serve in your favourite soup bowls and garnish with the fried almonds and melted mint butter.

Shish barak yoghurt soup (page 151)
Opposite page, top to bottom: Laban immo (page 153), Yoghurt noodle soup (page 152)

KHORESHT GHORMEH SABZI

This khoresht (Persian curry) of lamb and a tonne of herbs (sabzi) is normally served with red kidney beans topped with French fries. My version isn't, but by all means you can add the extras. This was on the menu when we first opened and it even managed to impress some of my Iranian friends.

Season the lamb with salt and seal in a heavy-based saucepan over a high heat until browned all over. Work in batches to ensure you maintain a high heat in the saucepan. Remove and set aside. In the same saucepan, heat the oil. Add the onion and garlic and cook until caramelised quite darkly (the onion should be the colour of chocolate) – this could take 30 minutes.

Add the finely chopped herbs and stir through, allowing the moisture of the herbs to 'deglaze', or release, the caramelised onion from the bottom. Stir for a few minutes then add the advieh and stir for another few minutes. Add 250 ml (1 cup) water to continue the process of deglazing. Stir again.

Return the lamb to the saucepan, stir through the herbs and onion, then add enough water to come to just below the meat. Turn the heat up to medium–high.

The liquid will appear to be boiling quite quickly but you should stir it all a few more times until the meat has warmed through enough to achieve a steady boil. When you are getting a consistent boil, turn the heat down to a low simmer and cover the saucepan with a lid. Cook until the lamb is soft and easy to cut with a spoon, about 2 hours. Give it a stir every 10 minutes or so for the first 30 minutes and ensure the khoresht is simmering gently.

Serves 6–8

1 kg (2 lb 4 oz) lamb shoulder, cut into 10 cm (4 in) chunks

salt, to season

2 tablespoons vegetable oil

2 onions, grated or blended in a food processor

2 garlic cloves, grated

1 bunch of flat-leaf parsley, finely chopped

1 bunch of coriander (cilantro), finely chopped

½ bunch of mint leaves, finely chopped

2 tablespoons Advieh (page 24)

Note
Stir often, being sure to scrape the bottom of the pot well, to ensure nothing sticks and burns.
Consider using a pressure cooker for this recipe and follow the manufacturer's instructions. The process will be different from that described above, but the ingredients will be the same.

THE ALBANIAN CHICKEN LIVERS THAT RENÉ REDZEPI LOVED

Albanian livers are a popular Turkish preparation of lamb liver that is finished with the classic combination of sumac, parsley and red onions. I don't particularly like lamb liver, so we had this dish on the menu with chicken livers instead. Ben Shewry had recommended that René Redzepi and his team go to Rumi while they were here for the Melbourne Food and Wine Festival and they tried (and loved) this dish. The icing on the cake was when René told me that he particularly enjoyed the livers because his father is Albanian.

Serves 4

200 g (7 oz) chicken livers, connective tissue removed
1 teaspoon Baharat (page 24)
½ teaspoon salt
2 tablespoons vegetable oil
¼ red onion, very finely sliced
4 flat-leaf parsley sprigs, leaves picked and finely shredded
1 teaspoon ground sumac
pinch of salt flakes
lemon wedges, to serve

Marinate the chicken livers with the baharat and salt. Set aside.

Heat the oil in a heavy-based frying pan over a high heat. When the oil begins to smoke, carefully add the chicken livers to the pan, trying not to overcrowd it.

Maintain a high heat and cook for 1 minute, then turn and cook for another minute.

Remove from the pan and rest on a plate for 2 minutes.

Mix the onion, parsley and sumac with a pinch of salt flakes.

Place the livers on a plate and top with the onion salad. Serve with lemon wedges on the side.

Q. Why are they called Albanian livers if they are Turkish?
A. The Ottoman Empire ruled over Albania for about 400 years, during which time a lot of cross-cultural exchange took place. There doesn't seem to be a definitive story, but it is said that the dish came from the many Albanian butchers in Istanbul.

AL SIKBAAJ

With the Middle East in the mess that it's in, it is easy to assume that it has always been like that. This recipe offers a chance to reflect on a time when the roles of Europe and the Middle East were more or less reversed: the Middle Ages, often considered the Dark Ages in Europe. Europe was poor and fractured and full of religious fervour while the Middle East was flourishing, making advancements in culture, the sciences and, importantly, food.

This recipe was inspired by a book called Medieval Arab Cookery, which was a series of manuscripts translated by Maxime Rodinson and Charles Perry. It was this book that sparked my interest in Persian cuisine, as I started to realise that many Middle Eastern dishes had Persian influences. Many of the cooks in Baghdad were Persian, and their influence on the Caliphate spread with the Islamic culture across the north of Africa and into Spain.

This dish, or, more accurately, the preparation method, caught my attention when I realised that escabeche, a well-known Spanish dish, had spread with Spanish conquest as far as Jamaica, South America (ceviche) and the Philippines. Ultimately, it is a dish that is served cold, marinated in saffron, vinegar and oil. Some original recipes also call for honey.

The recipe that follows is for the sauce. The main ingredient can be anything from classic fish fillets to steamed carrots.

Heat the olive oil in a saucepan over a medium heat. Add the onion with a pinch of salt and sweat for a minute or so before adding the garlic. Turn the heat down to low and cook for a further 3–4 minutes to soften the onion and garlic.

Add the saffron water and turn the heat back up to medium–high. Stir in the honey then gradually add the vinegar, stirring constantly. Remove from the heat and allow to cool.

Place your main ingredient on a plate, pour the sauce over the top and allow to marinate for at least half an hour.

Serve topped with the coriander leaves.

50 ml (1¾ fl oz) extra-virgin olive oil

1 red onion, sliced

pinch of salt

2 garlic cloves, finely sliced

2 tablespoons Saffron water (page 47)

1 teaspoon honey

1 tablespoon white wine vinegar

handful of coriander (cilantro) leaves

Options for the 'main' ingredient

250 g (9 oz) small fish fillets (a rich variety, such as sardine or mullet, pan-fried)

300 g (10½ oz) small carrots, steamed or roasted

1 eggplant (aubergine), sliced into 2 cm (¾ in) thick rounds and deep-fried until dark brown

leftover roast lamb, finely sliced

SŌNDWISHÉ

'Bidak sōndwishé?' Do you want a sandwich? Is there a sweeter question from your mum or aunty? I can't ever remember saying no – they sure kept me going. And the best of these, in my opinion, is the Lebanese flatbread sandwich. The sōndwishé. Arrous. Laffé. They are the perfect ratio of bread to filling: just enough to encase the ingredients you desire. My favourites growing up were labne and green olives; za'atar and olive oil; Smashed egg (page 61); sheep's feta and black olive; salami and 'plastic' cheese, and the guilty pleasure of cream cheese.

You may have noticed the absence of a quintessential Australian sandwich filling – Vegemite. Well, we thought it was disgusting growing up. That said, when you marry a 'Skip' and your little half-Skip son Patrick constantly smells like Vegemite crackers, your heart melts and you start to find that disgusting black paste a little more appealing. I often giggle to myself now when I push aside the jar of za'atar in favour of the Vegemite. Love rules.

ROAST CHICKEN
Tahini chicken (see page 133)
Soused onions (page 34)
Shredded parsley and lettuce
Fried almonds (see page 41)

SHREDDED LAMB
Shredded lamb shoulder (see page 128)
Shredded parsley
Labne (page 31)
Harissa (page 36)
Pickles (see page 72)

CAULIFLOWER
Fried cauliflower with caramelised onion, currants and pine nuts (page 94)
Almond taratoor (page 85)
Fried almonds (see page 41)

TOMATO FATTOUSH IN A SANDWICH (SEE PAGE 119)

JOE'S QUICK-FIXES
Sheep's feta and black olives
Labne (page 31) and green olives
Vegemite and cheese
Pistachio halva and honey

DRINKS

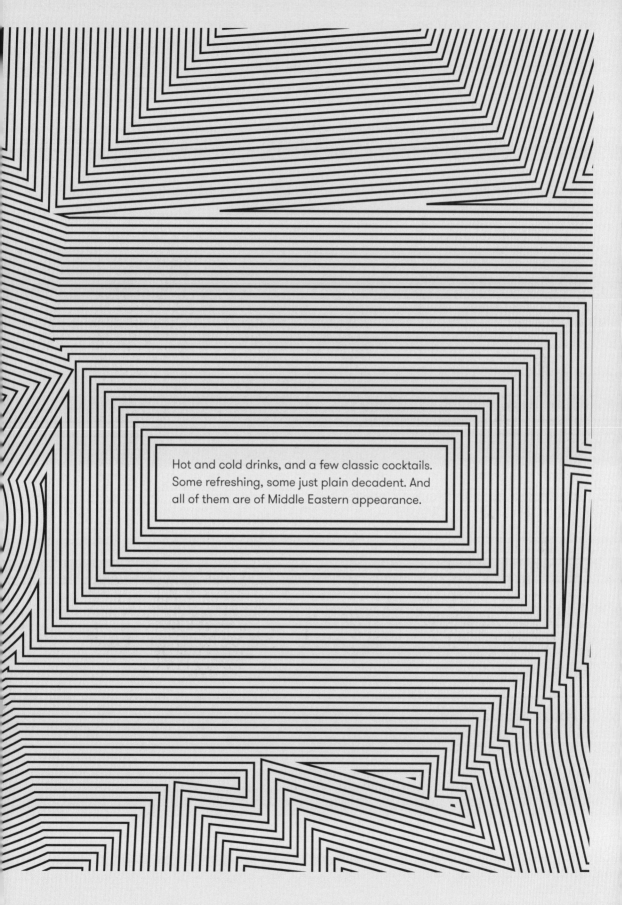

Hot and cold drinks, and a few classic cocktails. Some refreshing, some just plain decadent. And all of them are of Middle Eastern appearance.

ARABIC/LEBANESE/ TURKISH/GREEK COFFEE

Lebanese coffee is made using Turkish coffee. Confused? Well, the style of the roast and grind is considered Turkish, but Lebanese coffee differs in its preparation. Whereas the Turkish (and Greek) prefer 'crema' on top, most Lebanese boil away the crema, creating a shiny black brew. The addition of ground cardamom is also common in the Middle East.

Be aware that the coffee will double its height during the cooking process, so choose an appropriately sized pot.

Place 400 ml (14 fl oz) water in a small saucepan or Middle Eastern coffee pot (raqwa) with a spout and bring to the boil.

Remove from the heat and add the coffee, and sugar and cardamom if using.

Return to the heat and watch it very closely as the coffee will boil up and over to almost double its height if left unchecked. The idea now is to play the coffee boiling game that involves boiling the coffee up until it's just about to boil over then removing it from the heat and gently stirring the foam on top, then repeating the process until the foam 'breaks' and the coffee boils very black and shiny. Allow it to settle for a minute or so before serving, leaving the 'mud' in the bottom of the coffee pot. You should leave the mud in the bottom of your cup, too (unless of course you like that sort of thing).

Serves 4

100 g (3⅓ oz) ground Turkish coffee

1 tablespoon white (granulated) sugar (optional)

¼ teaspoon ground green cardamom (optional)

Lebanese cardamom iced coffee

There is no such thing as a Lebanese iced coffee, we just made it up by using excess coffee that we had left over from the day before, and it's a winner.

Make the cardamom coffee using the recipe above, but add an extra heaped tablespoon of coffee and 1 teaspoon of sugar. Allow to cool, then place in the fridge to chill.

The coffee sediment will completely settle overnight so it will be easy to pour the clear coffee brew off the top. Pour some of this into a glass with some ice and cold milk in whatever ratio you like.

Serves 4

1 × quantity Lebanese cardamom coffee (see above)

LEBANESE LEMONADE

· Recipes pictured on page 170

In a large container, mix the lemon halves and the sugar. Massage the sugar into the lemons with your hands or an improvised muddle stick until the mixture becomes soft and aromatic and the sugar is well rubbed into the lemons. Rest in the fridge for 24 hours until the sugar dissolves completely, the lemons soften a little and a syrup has formed.

Strain the whole mixture through a fine-mesh sieve, retaining the liquid, and return the lemons to the container. Add 250 ml (1 cup) water to the container and massage the lemons again to squeeze out all the goodness. Strain the mixture for a second time, reserving the liquid, then combine the juices from the first and second strain. Discard the lemons.

Stir in the orange-blossom water. You will now have about 500 ml (2 cups) concentrate.

To serve, add some ice to a glass with 125 ml (½ cup) lemonade and top up with water or soda to your taste.

You could add a little vodka or triple sec and some fresh mint and lemon slices for a boozy summer cocktail.

Serves 4, or makes 500 ml (2 cups) concentrate

4 unwaxed lemons, washed and halved

110 g (½ cup) white (granulated) sugar

1 teaspoon orange-blossom water

ice, to serve

30 ml (1 fl oz) vodka or triple sec (optional)

fresh mint leaves, to serve (optional)

lemon slices, to serve (optional)

HIBISCUS ICED TEA

Serves 8–10

50 g (1 cup) dried hibiscus flower (Karkade)

2 litres (8 cups) boiling water

110 g (½ cup) white (granulated) sugar

ice, to serve

30 ml (1 fl oz) gin (optional)

lime slice, to serve (optional)

Place the hibiscus in a saucepan with the boiling water and boil for a few minutes.

Remove from the heat, add the sugar, stirring to dissolve, then let the hibiscus steep for around 30 minutes. Allow to cool and refrigerate until chilled.

Serve with lots of ice on a hot day. You can add a 30 ml (1 fl oz) shot of gin and a slice of fresh lime to each glass to spice things up if you like.

ARAK

· Recipe pictured on page 175

Arak is a clear grape-based spirit that is distilled with aniseed and served mixed with water. A little like Greek ouzo, but better and stronger of course because it's Lebanese. It's always exciting to serve because the spirit starts out clear then turns milky white when you add water.

Arak is often introduced to a novice with a cheeky grin and the story of 'lion's or tiger's' milk. Or how it will put hairs on your chest. Or how you test it by igniting it. Sadly, many of these introductions are made with dodgy home brew that ensures the novice never becomes an expert. One sip normally sets their face on fire while the dad or uncle responsible stands by feeling vindicated.

Luckily, there are many distillers now in Lebanon and around the Middle East that are giving this drink the respect it deserves. They're using the best ingredients and are committed to quality and flavour. Some go on to mature the arak in clay amphora for years to ensure the arak is smooth to drink and the best flavours are highlighted. It turns out that good arak has nothing to do with lions or tigers.

Mix one-part arak with two-parts water, only adding ice after the water, as ice added directly to arak freezes the fennel seed oil, causing the arak to split.

AYRAN

Serves 4, or makes 1 litre (4 cups)

500 ml (2 cups) ice-cold water
500 g (1 lb 2 oz) natural yoghurt
1 teaspoon sea salt
ice, to serve
dried mint, to garnish

Whisk the water into the yoghurt and season with the salt.

Serve over ice and garnish with a pinch of dried mint. This is a drink best served very cold.

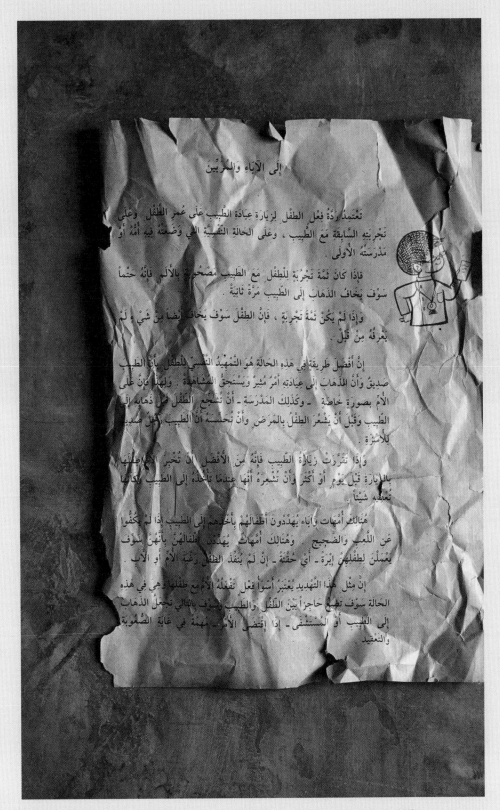

إلى الآباء والمربين

تَعْتَمِدُ رَدَّةُ فِعْلِ الطِّفْلِ لِزِيارَةِ عِيادَةِ الطَّبِيبِ عَلى عُمْرِ الطِّفْلِ وَعَلى
تَجْرِبَتِهِ السَّابِقَةِ مَعَ الطَّبِيبِ ، وَعَلى الحالَةِ النَّفْسِيَّةِ الَّتي وَضَعَتْهُ فيهِ أُمُّهُ أَوْ
مَدْرَسَتُهُ الأُولى .

فَإِذا كانَ ثَمَّةَ تَجْرِبَةٌ لِلطِّفْلِ مَعَ الطَّبِيبِ مَصْحُوبَةٌ بِالأَلَمِ فَإِنَّهُ حَتْماً
سَوْفَ يَخافُ الذَّهابَ إلى الطَّبِيبِ مَرَّةً ثانِيَةً .

وَإِذا لَمْ يَكُنْ ثَمَّةَ تَجْرِبَةٍ ، فَإِنَّ الطِّفْلَ سَوْفَ يَخافُ أَيْضاً مِنْ شَيْءٍ لَمْ
يَعْرِفْهُ مِنْ قَبْلُ .

إِنَّ أَفْضَلَ طَرِيقَةٍ في هذِهِ الحالَةِ هُوَ التَّمْهِيدُ النَّفْسِيُّ لِلطِّفْلِ بِأَنَّ الطَّبِيبَ
صَدِيقٌ وَأَنَّ الذَّهابَ إلى عِيادَتِهِ أَمْرٌ مُثيرٌ وَيَسْتَحِقُّ المُشاهَدَةَ . وَلِهذا فَإِنَّ عَلى
الأُمِّ بِصُورَةٍ خاصَّةٍ ـ وَكَذلِكَ المَدْرَسَةِ ـ أَنْ تُشَجِّعَ الطِّفْلَ عَلى ذَهابِهِ إلى
الطَّبِيبِ وَقَبْلَ أَنْ يَشْعُرَ الطِّفْلُ بِالمَرَضِ وَأَنْ تُحَسِّنَهُ أَنَّ الطَّبِيبَ مِثْلُ صَدِيقٍ
لِلأُسْرَةِ .

وَإِذا تَقَرَّرَتْ زِيارَةُ الطَّبِيبِ فَإِنَّهُ مِنَ الأَفْضَلِ أَنْ تُخْبِرَ الأُمُّ طِفْلَها
بِالزِّيارَةِ قَبْلَ يَوْمٍ أَوْ أَكْثَرَ وَأَنْ تُشْعِرَهُ أَنَّها عِنْدَما تَأْخُذُهُ إلى الطَّبِيبِ وَكَأَنَّها
تَمْنَحُهُ شَيْئاً .

هُنالِكَ أُمَّهاتٌ وَآباءٌ يُهَدِّدُونَ أَطْفالَهُمْ بِأَخْذِهِمْ إلى الطَّبِيبِ إذا لَمْ يَكُفُّوا
عَنِ اللَّعِبِ وَالضَّجِيجِ وَهُنالِكَ أُمَّهاتٌ يُهَدِّدْنَ أَطْفالَهُنَّ بِأَنَّهُنَّ سَوْفَ
يَعْمَلْنَ لِطِفْلِهِنَّ إِبْرَةً ـ أَيَّ حُقْنَةً ـ إِنْ لَمْ يُنَفِّذِ الطِّفْلُ رَغْبَةَ الأُمِّ أَوِ الأَبِ .

إِنَّ مِثْلَ هذا التَّهْدِيدِ يُعْتَبَرُ أَسْوَأَ فِعْلٍ تَفْعَلُهُ الأُمُّ مَعَ طِفْلِها وَهِيَ في هذِهِ
الحالَةِ سَوْفَ تَضَعُ حاجِزاً بَيْنَ الطِّفْلِ وَالطَّبِيبِ وَسَوْفَ بِالتّالي تَجْعَلُ الذَّهابَ
إلى الطَّبِيبِ أَوِ المُسْتَشْفى ـ إِذا اقْتَضى الأَمْرُ ـ مُهِمَّةً في غايَةِ الصُّعُوبَةِ
وَالتَّعْقِيدِ .

Opposite page, from top: Hibiscus iced tea (page 168), Lebanese lemonade (page 168)

RUMI COCKTAIL

· Recipes pictured on page 174

Place the sugar in a small saucer as wide as the rim of your glass. Rub a wedge of lime around the rim of your glass and tip it upside down in the sugar, ensuring that you get an even coating of sugar on the rim.

Fill the glass with ice cubes, then add the vodka and pomegranate juice.

Garnish with the other lime wedge.

Serves 1

1 tablespoon caster (superfine) sugar
2 lime wedges
ice, to serve
30 ml (1 fl oz) vodka
200 ml (7 fl oz) pomegranate juice

TURKISH DELIGHT MARTINI

Serves 1

1 teaspoon sugar syrup (see page 183)
1 tablespoon cocoa powder
30 ml (1 fl oz) vodka
1 teaspoon crème de cacao
1 teaspoon Monin rose syrup (not rose water)
ice, for shaking
edible rose petals, to garnish

Put the sugar syrup and cocoa powder in separate saucers and dip the rim of the glass first in the syrup, then in the cocoa powder to coat.

Pour the vodka, crème de cacao and rose syrup over the ice in your cocktail shaker. Shake for a minimum of 30 seconds (your drink should be opaque). Strain into the glass and garnish with edible rose petals.

LEBANESE CARDAMOM COFFEE AND VODKA MARTINI

Serves 1

30 ml (1 fl oz) vodka
60 ml (¼ cup) cold sweet
  Lebanese cardamom iced
  coffee (page 166)
15 ml (½ fl oz) coffee liqueur
ice, for shaking
pinch of ground green
  cardamom, to garnish

Shake all the ingredients in a cocktail shaker with ice for a minimum of 30 seconds to make sure it's foamy, then strain into a martini glass. Garnish with a pinch of ground cardamom.

SULTAN'S NEGRONI

· Recipes pictured on page 175

To make the ice block, place a small sprig of thyme in each mould of an extra-large ice-cube tray, making sure the ice blocks will fit in your tumbler.

Add 1 teaspoon saffron water to each mould, then top up with fresh water. Freeze overnight.

To make the drink, place an ice block in your favourite old-fashioned tumbler. Add the spirits to a mixing glass with ice and stir for 20–30 seconds. Strain over your saffron ice cube.

Spritz the orange-blossom water over the rim of the glass, then garnish with a slice of fresh orange.

Serves 1

1 Saffron and thyme ice block
  (see below)
30 ml (1 fl oz) Campari
30 ml (1 fl oz) sweet
  vermouth
30 ml (1 fl oz) gin
ice, for mixing
orange-blossom water in a
  spray bottle, for spritzing
1 fresh orange slice, to garnish

Saffron and thyme ice block
a few fresh thyme sprigs
Saffron water (page 47)

Left to right:
Lebanese cardamom
coffee and vodka
martini (page 173),
Rumi cocktail
(page 172), Turkish
delight martini
(page 173), Sultan's
negroni (page 172),
Arak (page 169)

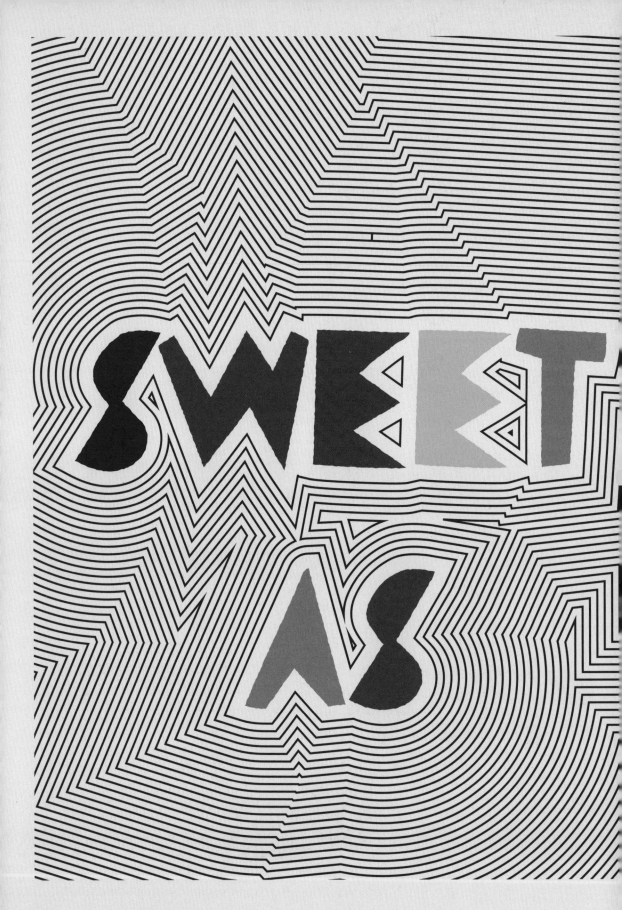

Sweet as habibi. Middle Eastern sweets are really sweet. Considered less of a dessert and more of a treat with coffee or tea, they're a part of the menu that has always been a challenge for me to place in the context of a modern restaurant. I have often found a couple of sweet mouthfuls of a labne-filled date or a piece of Turkish delight hits the spot just right after a big spread. But some of these desserts are pretty serious offerings, too.

MUHALLABIEH CHOCOLATE PUDDING WITH BARBERRIES AND POMEGRANATE

This version of a classic Lebanese milk pudding normally set with cornflour (cornstarch) is a rip off of Rita Macali's chocolate panna cotta. When working at Ladro as the prep chef before opening Rumi, I would occasionally sneak one of these for breakfast. Rita served it with raspberries. We serve it with barberries and pomegranate molasses. We also serve it in a glass with a couple of biscuits, darling.

Soak the barberries in water for at least 2 hours, then drain well. Mix with the pomegranate molasses and set aside.

To make the chocolate pudding, place the chocolate, milk, cream and sugar in a saucepan set over a low heat. Gently dissolve the chocolate, stirring occasionally, then bring almost to the boil. Quickly turn off the heat as soon as you see any sign of boiling.

While the chocolate pudding mixture is heating, submerge the gelatine leaf in water for about 5 minutes till it softens.

Remove the softened gelatine from the water, squeeze out any excess and place in the hot chocolate pudding mixture. Stir to thoroughly dissolve. Pour into glasses and set overnight in the fridge.

To serve, top with 1 teaspoon of the barberries and syrup and serve with your favourite biscuits.

Serves 8

50 g (1¾ oz) dried barberries
50 ml (1¾ fl oz) pomegranate molasses
80 g (2¾ oz) dark chocolate
90 ml (3 fl oz) full-cream milk
290 ml (10 fl oz) thick (double) cream
50 g (1¾ oz) caster (superfine) sugar
1 silver-grade gelatine leaf
sweet biscuits, to serve

LABNE-FILLED DATES

A large Middle Eastern meal is generally followed by small sweet treats and fresh fruit rather than a large dessert, hence the offering of sweet morsels that provide a little sugar hit. More elaborate sweets are a separate event either long after the meal or as standalone treats for a morning or afternoon catch-up, normally involving rich black coffee. These dates are a mainstay of the Rumi sweet treats menu. At the time of writing this, our dates were filled with labne, tahini, fig and sesame jam, and coffee. This recipe is inspired by the traditional version, which is often filled with a whole almond or half a walnut.

Remove the pits from the dates by making a small incision down the length of the date and carefully pulling out the pit. Make an effort to keep the dates in shape.

Prepare the filling by mixing the labne, tahini, jam and coffee powder together.

To fill the dates, you simply open them up at the slit and use a teaspoon or a piping bag to fill the date with the labne mixture.

If using sesame seeds, dip the top of the stuffed date into the sesame seeds before serving.

Makes 20

20 medjool dates

160 g (5¾ oz) unsalted Labne (page 31)

20 g (¾ oz) tahini

50 g (1¾ oz) fig and sesame jam (see Q&A)

½ teaspoon Lebanese coffee powder

10 g (¼ oz) toasted sesame seeds (optional)

Q. Where can I buy fig and sesame jam?
A. In Middle Eastern shops.
Q. Can I use other ingredients to fill the dates?
A. You can try this with plain labne or any other jams and nuts you have on hand.

Baklava Ice-cream Sandwich

· Recipe pictured on page 184

Rumi's baklava ice-cream sandwich was inspired by bastani, a Persian ice-cream sandwich made of saffron ice cream between two wafers.

It's quite a process to make this sandwich but well worth the effort. I recommend making it over two or three days to give you plenty of time to enjoy the process. Firstly, you will need to make the cinnamon milk and allow it to cool. Then you make the ice cream base and allow it to cool. Then you churn the ice cream. You can bake the pastry and toast the macadamias on any of these days. You can also make the syrup days in advance.

FOR THE CINNAMON MILK

Place the butter and cinnamon in a saucepan set over a low heat and stir occasionally until the butter has melted then browned. Be careful not to let the butter burn.

Remove the saucepan from the heat, add the milk and stir occasionally while the mixture cools to room temperature. Refrigerate overnight. The mixture will split as it cools, giving you cinnamon-infused butter sitting on top of flavoured milk. When completely cold, remove the butter from the top of the milk, setting it aside to be clarified, and strain the milk through a fine-mesh sieve to remove the cinnamon. Discard the cinnamon pieces.

Time to clarify the butter. Place the cinnamon-infused butter in a saucepan over a low heat and allow it to melt without stirring. This allows the pure fat (ghee), which looks like a clear yellow liquid, to separate from the milk solids, which will sink to the bottom of the saucepan. Once the milk solids have sunk, slowly and gently pour off the ghee, carefully leaving the solids behind.

Set aside the ghee to use for the pastry. Discard the solids.

TO MAKE THE ICE CREAM

Whisk the yolks and sugar in a stand mixer for 5 minutes on high speed till it is the consistency of yoghurt.

In a saucepan, whisk together the cinnamon and almond milks with the cream, then bring to the boil with the sahlep, honey, glucose and a tiny pinch of salt.

Next we temper the sweetened egg yolks by placing a small amount (about one-fifth) of the hot baklava milk base into the cold egg mixture, whisking constantly so the eggs don't scramble. Slowly add the rest of the hot milk base until all the milk is mixed thoroughly into the eggs.

Serves 12

Cinnamon milk
250 g (9 oz) butter

20 g (¾ oz) cinnamon sticks, lightly crushed into large chunks

400 ml (14 fl oz) full-cream milk

Baklava ice cream
4 egg yolks

60 g (2¼ oz) caster (superfine) sugar

100 ml (3½ fl oz) Cinnamon milk (see method)

100 ml (3½ fl oz) almond milk

40 g (1½ oz) thick (double) cream

2 g (¹⁄₁₆ oz) sahlep powder (see Note), or pinch of cornflour (cornstarch)

10 g (¼ oz) honey

10 g (¼ oz) liquid glucose

pinch of salt

Sugar syrup

150 g (5½ oz) caster (superfine) sugar

1 teaspoon orange-blossom water

2 teaspoons lemon juice

Baklava pastry

30 sheets filo pastry

60 g (2¼ oz) cinnamon ghee (see method, opposite)

100 ml (3½ fl oz) Sugar syrup (see above)

Ground cinnamon, for dusting

Macadamias

50 g (1¾ oz) macadamia nuts

1 teaspoon cinnamon ghee, melted (see method, opposite)

Return to the saucepan and cook gently till the mixture reaches 82°C (180°F) on a cooking thermometer. Stir constantly.

Remove from the heat and allow to cool. Follow your ice-cream machine instructions to churn the ice cream. You want a smooth, creamy ice cream. Place in the freezer until you are ready to assemble the ice-cream sandwich.

PREPARE A SUGAR SYRUP

Place the sugar in a saucepan with 50 ml (1¾ fl oz) water. Stir over a low heat to dissolve the sugar, then bring to the boil. Remove from the heat as soon as it boils, then add the orange-blossom water and lemon juice. Allow to cool to room temperature.

FOR THE BAKLAVA PASTRY

Preheat the oven to 140°C (275°F).

Remove the pastry from the packet and lay flat. Cut the sheets in half and stack on top of one another. Cut out squares approximately 5 × 5 cm (2 × 2 in) and lay each pile snugly on a baking tray that will hold the piles of pastry covered in melted ghee. Each pile will become the top and the bottom of your ice-cream sandwich.

Melt the ghee in a saucepan then pour it evenly over the pastry. The pastry will be saturated. Bake for approximately 40 minutes, or until golden brown. Remove from the oven and immediately drizzle with the sugar syrup, coating the pastry evenly. Set aside to make the sandwiches later. Increase the oven temperature to 180°C (350°F).

FOR THE MACADAMIA NUTS

Lastly, coat the macadamia nuts with the ghee in a baking tray and toast in the oven for about 20 minutes, or until lightly browned. Allow to cool, then roughly crush with a mortar and pestle. You don't want a fine powder, so don't crush too much.

To assemble, separate the filo pastry squares, creating a top and bottom pile.

Place the bottom pile of filo on a serving plate, then top with a large scoop of ice cream. Make a small indent on the top of the ice cream, place 1 teaspoon of the crushed macadamias into the indent, then place the remaining pastry pile on top. Dust with a little ground cinnamon to serve.

Note
Sahlep powder is available from Middle Eastern grocers.

Christmas fruit mince ma'mool (page 187)
Opposite page: Baklava ice-cream sandwich (pages 182–3)

CHRISTMAS FRUIT MINCE MA'MOOL

I was very excited when I came up with this idea. It was around Christmas time when some fruit mince pies caught my eye because they looked like misshapen ma'mool. I couldn't get past the idea of a cross-cultural biscuit that represented my world: a Lebanese man married to an Australian woman with three little mince ma'mool.

I love that the Anglo fruit mince Christmas tart and the ma'mool that appears at my Lebanese family Easter is also popular during the Lebanese Eid. You will need to start this recipe a few days in advance. You can find a beautiful ma'mool mould from a Middle Eastern grocer.

Makes 36

icing (confectioners') sugar,
  for dusting

Filling
125 g (4½ oz) brown sugar
100 g (3½ oz) raisins
1 apple, grated
50 g (1¾ oz) barberries
juice and zest of 1 orange
50 g (1¾ oz) medjool dates,
  pitted and chopped
50 g (1¾ oz) dried figs, chopped
50 g (1¾ oz) currants
50 ml (1¾ fl oz) muscat
1½ tablespoons almond meal
50 g (1¾ oz) ghee, melted
pinch of ground nutmeg
pinch of ground cloves
pinch of ground ginger

Pastry
720 g (4 cups) fine semolina
300 g (2 cups) plain
  (all-purpose) flour
600 g (1 lb 5 oz) butter, melted
½ teaspoon baking powder
2 teaspoons orange-blossom
  water or rose water
60 g (2¼ oz) caster (superfine)
  sugar
150 ml (5 fl oz) warm
  full-cream milk

For the filling, place all the ingredients in a bowl, mix well and refrigerate. This is best done a few days in advance.

To make the pastry, mix the semolina and flour well, then add the melted butter and mix thoroughly to ensure the flours are coated in the butter. Mix all the other ingredients separately, then add to the flour mixture, combining well. Bring together into a ball, wrap in plastic wrap and rest the dough in the fridge for 30 minutes.

Preheat your oven to 190°C (375°F). Line two baking trays with baking paper.

Remove the pastry from the fridge and divide into 36 balls, each about 45 g (1¾ oz).

Take a ball of pastry and use your fingers to press it into a small cup shape with a hollow a bit bigger than the size of a walnut. Fill the hollow with 1 teaspoon of the fruit mixture, then close the edges of the pastry over the mixture. Roll into a ball, ensuring that no fruit mince escapes, and put to one side. Continue until you have used all the pastry and filling. By the time you've finished you'll have worked out the best way for you to stuff the pastry; next time it will be so much easier!

Carefully but firmly press each ball into a ma'mool mould, flattening the base. Remove from the mould by turning it upside down and tapping the mould on your bench to release.

Place the ma'mool on the baking trays and bake for about 20 minutes, removing them as they begin to colour. Allow to cool then dust with icing sugar.

ARAK-POACHED APRICOTS FILLED WITH LABNE

These are delicious mouthfuls that hit the spot when you feel like you've eaten enough. The aniseed from the arak is a perfect match with the apricot, and the labne gives it a beautiful creamy, tart element.

Soak the dried apricots in water for 3 days to rehydrate.

Bring the sugar and 500 ml (2 cups) water to the boil in a saucepan and stir over a medium–low heat until the sugar has dissolved.

Add the lemon, orange, cardamom and 1½ teaspoons of the arak and bring back to the boil.

Drain the soaked apricots and discard the water.

Add the apricots to the syrup, bring to the boil and simmer over a very low heat for 20 minutes.

Allow to cool, then refrigerate with all the flavourings left in the syrup. (They will keep in the fridge for up to 10 weeks.)

To serve, remove the apricots from the syrup and place on a plate. Stir the remaining ½ teaspoon arak into the labne. Open the slit in the apricots and spoon or pipe in the labne.

Serves 8–10

250 g (9 oz) dried whole apricots, stones removed

250 g (9 oz) caster (superfine) sugar

1 lemon, peeled and halved

1 orange, peeled and halved

1 teaspoon green cardamom pods, lightly pounded

2 teaspoons arak

50 g (1¾ oz) unsalted Labne (page 31)

Q. What do I do with the leftover syrup?
A. I'm glad you asked. Strain the flavourings then boil the liquid till it is reduced to a thick syrup that can be drizzled over any number of foods, such as vanilla ice cream or cake.

RICE PUDDING BRÛLÉE

This is a riff on a classic Turkish rice pudding, which actually caramelises naturally when baked. I coat the surface with sugar and brûlée the top either by blowtorching or grilling it. This dish can be served warm or cold.

Serves 6–8

220 g (1 cup) short-grain rice

70 g (2½ oz) caster (superfine) sugar, plus a little extra for the brulée

1.2 litres (5 cups) full-cream milk

6 green cardamom pods, cracked

1 cinnamon stick

zest of 1 lemon

Place all the ingredients in a heavy-based saucepan and bring to the boil over a medium heat. Stir all the way to the bottom and into the corners to make sure it doesn't stick.

Once the mixture begins to boil, turn down the heat and keep stirring until it thickens to the consistency of custard.

Remove from the pan and spoon in glass or ceramic bowls that can withstand the heat of a grill or blowtorch. Sprinkle with an even coating of sugar, then use a blowtorch or place under a very hot grill to caramelise the tops.

ALMOND PUDDING

A sweet Turkish milk pudding made with almond meal. I like to serve this with an Iranian sour cherry jam, but you can also try it with your own favourite jam.

Place all the ingredients, except the jam and pistachios (if using), in a heavy-based saucepan and bring to the boil over a medium heat. Stir all the way to the bottom and into the corners so it doesn't stick.

Once the mixture begins to boil, reduce the heat to low and keep stirring until it thickens to the consistency of custard.

Remove from the heat and place in a bowl or container, cover, and chill in the fridge.

When ready to serve, spoon into serving bowls and top with sour cherry jam, or your favourite jam or stewed fruit. Sprinkle with the chopped pistachios, if using.

Serves 4

100 g (1 cup) almond meal

25 g (1 oz) rice flour

85 g (3 oz) caster (superfine) sugar

500 ml (2 cups) full-cream milk

jam of your choice, or stewed fruit, to serve

2 tablespoons chopped pistachio kernels, to garnish (optional)

TURKISH DELIGHT MARIE BISCUIT SANDWICHES

This is more of a delicious, clever idea than a recipe. I became familiar with this combination when my sister-in-law, Lulu, would make these biscuit sandwiches at the end of a family lunch during Lent when half of the family refrain from all animal products, including butter and cream that are in most delicious things.

Makes 1

Turkish delight
2 Marie or other sweet
  biscuits

Take a piece of the softest Turkish delight you can find and sandwich between two Marie biscuits.

Serve with strong black Lebanese coffee (see page 166).

NAT'S ROCKY ROAD TO DAMASCUS

The whole of the Abboud family is absolutely mad for chocolate. Come to think of it, almost every chef I've ever met is also mad for chocolate. This is my wife's recipe for a pimped-up version of rocky road that we sometimes make at the restaurant.

Start by melting the chocolate in a heatproof bowl set over a saucepan of gently simmering water.

Line a large baking tray with baking paper.

In a large bowl, combine the desiccated coconut, pistachios and barberries.

Cut the honeycomb, Turkish delight and marshmallows into quarters. Add to the bowl and toss until well combined.

Pour in the melted chocolate and mix well, then tip onto the baking paper and flatten out to your preferred thickness (I make it about 3 cm/1¼ in thick). You can top with some extra chopped pistachio kernels and some edible dried rose petals if you like.

Refrigerate until set, then chop into chunks and serve. Store in the fridge or in a cool, dark place – but it won't last long!

Serves 10–15

500 g (1 lb 2 oz) dark chocolate

25 g (¼ cup) desiccated coconut

100 g (¾ cup) pistachio kernels, plus extra for topping (optional)

50 g (1¾ oz) barberries

100 g (3½ oz) chocolate-coated honeycomb

200 g (7 oz) Turkish delight, ideally rose

100 g (3½ oz) marshmallows

edible dried rose petals, for topping (optional)

TURKA MI SU

This recipe was developed by a longstanding friend, Trina Fazio, and the team at Moor's Head made it an 'inauthentic' tiramisu. I didn't think the Italian version could get any better, but the addition of the cardamom and pistachios takes it to the next level.

Serves 12

4 eggs, separated

180 g (6½ oz) caster (superfine) sugar

1 teaspoon ground cardamom

250 g (9 oz) mascarpone

500 ml (2 cups) Lebanese (Turkish) cardamom coffee (see page 166)

60 ml (¼ cup) Marsala or coffee liqueur

500 g (1 lb 2 oz) sponge finger biscuits

100 g (3½ oz) cocoa powder

100 g (¾ cup) finely chopped pistachio kernels

To make a sabayon, whisk the egg yolks, sugar and ground cardamom in a mixer on high speed until thick and pale.

In a large bowl, stir the mascarpone until smooth and softened. Gradually add the sabayon to the mascarpone.

In a clean bowl, whisk the egg whites until stiff peaks form. Gently fold the stiff egg whites through the mascarpone mixture to make a light custard.

Combine the coffee and liqueur in a separate shallow dish and soak the sponge finger biscuits in the coffee mix. Gently squeeze any excess liquid from the biscuits and place flat on the bottom of a serving dish. Cover the biscuits with a layer of the custard. Repeat these layers twice with a smaller amount of custard on top. Smooth over with a spatula and refrigerate for at least a couple of hours.

Serve dusted generously with the cocoa powder and finish with chopped pistachios.

Note
This recipe uses raw eggs so make sure they're fresh and keep your turka mi su refrigerated.

Q. I don't have any Turkish coffee, can I use espresso?
A. Yes, you can. Feel free to use whichever coffee you prefer, just be sure to make it strong!

لزيارة عادة الط...
الحالة الص...

...رية للطفل مع الطبي...
الطبيب مرة ثانية...

...رية، فإن الطفل سوف يح...

...ده الحالة هو التمهيد الت...
أمرٌ مثير ويستحي ال...
المدرسة - أن تنج...
المريض وأن تحس...

الطبيب فإنه من الأف...
وأن تشعرُه أنها عندما...

...ـات وآباء يُهدِّدونَ أطفالهُم بأخ... وهنالك أمهات يه...
...والضجيج.

يعملنَ لطفلهِن إبرة - أي حُقنة - إن لَم يُنفذ
إن مِثل هذا التهديد يُعتبر أسوأ فعل تف...
الحالة سوف تضع حاجزاً بين الطفل والطبي...
إلى الطبيب أو المستشفى - إذا اقتضى ال...
والتعقيد.

ZNOUD EL SIT WITH BANANA AND HALVA

Znoud el sit translates to 'ladies' upper arms'. It is a large filo cigar filled with ashta. Ashta is a thick clotted cream used in Middle Eastern pastries that is made by accumulating the 'skin' of simmering milk. The addition of the banana and halva is inspired by memories of my father making banana and halva sandwiches.

Serves 6–8

10 g (¼ oz) butter

25 g (1 oz) brown sugar

1 small ripe banana, chopped into 1 cm (½ in) pieces

2 teaspoons lemon juice

500 g (1 lb 2 oz) ashta or fresh curd cheese, such as cottage cheese

50 g (1¾ oz) halva, crumbled

10 sheets thick filo pastry

oil, for deep-frying (see page 49)

Sugar syrup
750 g (1 lb 10 oz) white (granulated) sugar

50 ml (1¾ fl oz) orange-blossom water

50 ml (1¾ fl oz) lemon juice

Note
The traditional version of this recipe is made with ashta alone. Just leave out the banana and halva as an accompaniment. You could also substitute the bananas with some delicious overripe figs.

Q. Where can I buy ashta?
A. Most Middle Eastern sweet shops sell ashta. Alternatively, you can try making this recipe with ricotta or any other fresh curd cheese. If you want to have a go at making your own ashta, bring 1 litre (4 cups) full-cream milk to the boil in a wide saucepan, then turn the heat right down as low as it will go. The 'milk skin' will accumulate at the top of the pan. Lift the skin off the milk using a slotted spoon, and place it in a bowl. Repeat until almost all the milk is gone – this can take a few hours. Discard anything left in the pot.

Make the sugar syrup by placing the sugar in a saucepan with 250 ml (1 cup) water. Stir over a low heat to dissolve the sugar then bring to the boil. Switch off the heat as soon as it boils, then remove and add the orange-blossom water and lemon juice. Allow to cool to room temperature.

Place a small saucepan over a medium–high heat and heat the butter and brown sugar until it completely melts and begins to boil. Add the chopped banana and stir through the sugar.

Add the lemon juice and stir, then remove from the heat and allow to cool. Place in a bowl and fold through the ashta and halva.

Lay the pastry flat on a chopping board and cut into even strips approximately 10–12 cm (4–4½ in) wide. Place all the piles under a damp tea towel so they don't dry out as you make the individual znood.

To roll the pastries, place one piece of pastry vertically and one piece of pastry horizontally on your work surface, creating an upside-down cross.

Place a heaped tablespoon of the ashta mix in the middle of the horizontal piece, flattening the mix a little. Fold each end of the horizontal piece over to cover the mixture, then fold the bottom of the vertical piece up and over the ashta. Roll it all into a cigar shape, sealing the edge with a little water. It should be about as thick as a small banana. Set aside and repeat.

Heat enough oil for deep-frying in a large saucepan or deep-fryer to 180°C (350°F). Working in batches, deep-fry the znood for a couple of minutes until the edges are dark brown. Remove from the oil, drain well, then immediately dunk in the sugar syrup for about 30 seconds. Remove from the syrup, allowing any excess to drain away. Set aside on a tray until you're ready to serve.

THANK YOU

Cookbooks and restaurants have a key person that is normally given the spotlight but these projects never get anywhere without the hard work and support of so many people that nobody knows. It was challenging to separate the work various people put into the restaurant from the book. In this case, there would be no book without the restaurant and no restaurant without the following people.

First and foremost the biggest of thanks goes to my wife Nat who has been my greatest supporter and my rock through the best and the worst of the life of Rumi. Nat, you've been such a huge part of Rumi the restaurant and Rumi the book. From the early days of sounding out ideas for our future restaurant, to rolling up your sleeves for the countless hours of demolition, sanding, painting and cleaning to turn a vision into a reality. You took on the role of running the front of house with virtually no experience in doing so, but still ensuring everyone that walked through the door felt the love we were trying to give. At the points that I thought I couldn't take it anymore, you were there to get me over the line. When I just couldn't get my head around how I was going to test the recipes for this book you picked up the pieces to get me over the line once again.

To my dear Mum and Dad. I wish I could put into words (appropriate for this page) what you mean to me. Thanks for having the courage to search for a better life and enduring the hardship that comes with that. Thanks for the unconditional support even when you don't exactly know what the hell I'm doing. All that has been created at Rumi is built on the culture that you shared with me and that you left behind when you made the decision to leave Lebanon to create a brighter future for your next generation.

Thanks to my parents-in-law. Mem, the obvious thanks for the work you've done on the first edits of my words and recipes in this book. Thanks for respecting my voice as you helped shaped it. Thanks for all that you've contributed to Rumi weather it was making aprons to hanging curtains. Thanks to Terry for lending me your ear and guidance in the planning of Rumi and for the last 17 years of continued support. It has made a huge impact on me.

Thanks to my siblings who have helped in their own ways, whether it's filling in shifts, being a vocal supporter or just being test dummies for the potential car crashes I come up with.

There's a group of friends and family that I can never forget that did crucial building works at the original Rumi site when there was no budget for it. Without people like you, projects like Rumi can't get off the ground. I'm sure I've missed a couple but thanks Lorenzo, Peter, Ivan, Ky, Auntie Catherine and Auntie Jane.

Thanks to Jane Willson for believing in this book. Thanks for being in my corner as I fumbled my way through this process.

Thanks to Murdoch Books and the team that worked on this project. So many people are involved to bring a cookbook to life. Thanks to Armelle Habib, Lee Blaylock, Justin Wolfers, Andrea O'Connor, Kristy Allen and George Saad.

Thanks to Dani Valent for the generous foreword.

Thanks to the current and former staff of Rumi of the past 17 years, so many of whom left the place better than how they found it.

Thanks to a couple of the mentors that have been invaluable to me along the way, Tony Fazio and Mark Jackson.

Last but not least, a special thanks goes to the thousands and thousands of guests that have dined at Rumi since 2006. The restaurant is ultimately for you, and it's been a privilege to be a part of so many of your special times.

INDEX

Published in 2023 by Murdoch Books, an imprint of Allen & Unwin

Murdoch Books Australia
Cammeraygal Country
83 Alexander Street
Crows Nest NSW 2065
Phone: +61 (0)2 8425 0100
murdochbooks.com.au
info@murdochbooks.com.au

Murdoch Books UK
Ormond House
26–27 Boswell Street
London WC1N 3JZ
Phone: +44 (0) 20 8785 5995
murdochbooks.co.uk
info@murdochbooks.co.uk

For corporate orders and custom publishing, contact our business development team at
salesenquiries@murdochbooks.com.au

Publisher: Jane Willson
Editorial Manager: Justin Wolfers
Design Manager: Kristy Allen
Designer: George Saad
Editor: Andrea O'Connor
Photographer: Armelle Habib
Stylist: Lee Blaylock
Production Director: Lou Playfair

*Murdoch Books acknowledges the Traditional Owners of the Country on which we live and
work. We pay our respects to all Aboriginal and Torres Strait Islander Elders, past and present.*

ISBN 9 781 92261 644 9

 A catalogue record for this
book is available from the
National Library of Australia

A catalogue record for this book is available from the British Library

Colour reproduction by Splitting Image Colour Studio Pty Ltd, Wantirna, Victoria
Printed by 1010 Printing International Limited, China

OVEN GUIDE: You may find cooking times vary depending on the oven you are using. For fan-
forced ovens, as a general rule, set the oven temperature to 20°C (35°F) lower than indicated
in the recipe.

TABLESPOON MEASURES: We have used 20 ml (4 teaspoon) tablespoon measures. If you
are using a 15 ml (3 teaspoon) tablespoon add an extra teaspoon of the ingredient for each
tablespoon specified.

10 9 8 7 6 5 4 3 2 1